M000013970

The Better Way;
A Better Life

The Better Way;
A Better Life

A LIFE CHANGING JOURNEY
FOR CPAS & FINANCIAL ADVISORS

*On **Purpose**,*

*with **Passion**, by **Design***

HARRY PAPPAS, JR., CFP®

Inspired by Anthony P. Lombardi, Perfect Client

Copyright © 2014 by Harry Pappas, Jr.

All rights reserved. No part of this book may be used or reproduced in any manner whatsoever without prior written consent of the author, except as provided by the United States of America copyright law.

Published by Advantage, Charleston, South Carolina.
Member of Advantage Media Group.

ADVANTAGE is a registered trademark and the Advantage colophon is a trademark of Advantage Media Group, Inc.

Printed in the United States of America.

ISBN: 978-159932-491-3
LCCN: 2014937960

This publication is designed to provide accurate and authoritative information in regard to the subject matter covered. It is sold with the understanding that the publisher is not engaged in rendering legal, accounting, or other professional services. If legal advice or other expert assistance is required, the services of a competent professional person should be sought.

Advantage Media Group is proud to be a part of the Tree Neutral® program. Tree Neutral offsets the number of trees consumed in the production and printing of this book by taking proactive steps such as planting trees in direct proportion to the number of trees used to print books. To learn more about Tree Neutral, please visit **www.treeneutral.com**. To learn more about Advantage's commitment to being a responsible steward of the environment, please visit **www.advantagefamily.com/green**

Advantage Media Group is a publisher of business, self-improvement, and professional development books and online learning. We help entrepreneurs, business leaders, and professionals share their Stories, Passion, and Knowledge to help others Learn & Grow. Do you have a manuscript or book idea that you would like us to consider for publishing? Please visit **advantagefamily.com** or call **1.866.775.1696**.

ABOUT THE AUTHOR

 Harry Pappas Jr. is a CERTIFIED FINANCIAL PLANNER™ practitioner for a major bank and has been a financial advisor since 1985. Harry is the author of *The Better Way; A Better Life: A Life-Changing Journey for CPAs and Financial Advisors,* and president and CEO of the Pappas Media Group LLC. Harry has developed relationships with teams of CPAs, attorneys, and business-solution providers to bring the most innovative and integrated financial strategies to clients. His unique understanding of the accounting profession has positioned him as an expert and thought leader by reinventing the way CPAs serve their affluent business-owner clients and high-net-worth families. Harry is helping CPAs solve the distinct, immediate, and ongoing challenge of integrating wealth-management services into their practice.

Harry is a graduate of Florida State University and grew up in a small coal town 30 minutes from Pittsburgh, Pennsylvania. In only his third year, Harry was named to the Chairman's Council at Salomon Smith Barney. This honor is normally reserved for senior advisors. In 1991, in recognition of his dedication to his clients, commitment to quality and successful money management, Pappas was promoted to Vice President, Investments. Then in 1994, he was promoted to senior vice president and became a member of the firm's Director's Council, which is a top honor bestowed upon an advisor at Salomon Smith Barney.

Registered Representative magazine honored his success as it selected him as one of its "Top Ten Brokers" in 1996, an honor no individual can receive more than once. The selection criteria were based on superior performance in money management, client service, business building, and acknowledged peer recognition and respect. Shortly thereafter, he was invited to write a monthly column for the magazine, which he called "Selling from the Heart." As a follow-up to his column, he was asked to write a book explaining what is necessary to build a successful investment planning practice. In 2004, Pappas transitioned his business to Wachovia Securities, which subsequently was purchased by a major bank. Shortly after joining his new firm, Harry earned the firm's highest title. In June 2007, he became a Certified Estate and Trust Specialist (CES) awarded by the Institute of Business and Finance (IBF).

Pappas is a much-sought-after national speaker, sharing his success with colleagues, financial advisors, and investors. Whether he is leading a workshop or a seminar, or delivering a keynote speech, he puts his entire body, soul, and heart into a powerful message that he delivers with a fiery passion. In addition, he writes a biweekly financial column for his hometown newspaper, *The Ponte Vedra Recorder*. In July 2013, the National Association of Board Certified Advisory Practices (NABCAP) named his group one of North Florida's top premier wealth advisory practices. His accomplishments were featured in the August 2013 issue of *Jacksonville Magazine*.

Pappas employs a comprehensive, holistic, fee-based investment planning practice that offers a wide range of financial services that cover all areas of portfolio management. He represents clients in 30 states, where his team specializes in developing cohesive financial strategies to fit clients' specific needs.

He and his team are experienced, energized, educated, and informed. Their business philosophy is built on three cornerstones: honesty, integrity, and client service, and they have an emotional and intellectual commitment to be "the best game in town." Pappas's primary focus is on money management and estate-planning strategies for high-net-worth individuals, business owners, and professionals. He has established himself as one of the most respected advisors through a solid work ethic, conservative investment ideology, and a solid commitment to client service.

Harry, an insanely curious person and self-admitted perfectionist, is obsessed with personal and professional growth. Harry is not content with resting on his laurels; he is remarkably committed to continually searching for methods to accomplish things more quickly, more professionally, more cost effectively, and more efficiently. Harry's family, friends, and colleagues all agree that he doesn't know much about a lot of things, but what he does know, he knows exceptionally well. Ask Harry what his secret to success is and he quickly replies, "Passion! I have boundless enthusiasm and love for my work and I am driven by a burning desire to serve my clients. Furthermore, we offer total transparency, a set of values, and a code of conduct that we all respect and follow. For me, work is fun!"

Pappas and his family live in Ponte Vedra Beach, Florida. He balances his love for work with his love for his wife and two children, along with his passion for running. Harry and Vickie were married in 1987. They have a daughter, Tori, who is a public relations specialist with EverBank, and a son, Trey, who attends College of Charleston as a sophomore. Meet Harry at www.thebetterwayabetterlife.com.

ACKNOWLEDGEMENT

Sometimes in life we are fortunate to meet truly inspirational people. Let me tell you about four incredible people who live their lives with purpose, passion, and design so that they truly influence others' lives. Additionally, they embody what Earl Nightingale proclaimed in what could be the greatest motivational piece ever written, *The Strangest Secret: We Become What We Think About.* According to the author, what makes this a secret is that "very few people have learned it or understand it. That's why it's strange, and why for some equally strange reason it virtually remains a secret." Each of these people took their own path to success via a passion for the power to change lives. What makes them so special is their remarkable and passionate message of "influence." Each, in their own way, demonstrates that if we truly have a passion and purpose, then we can inspire and help others. They remind me of the words of Margaret Mead: "Never believe that a few caring people can't change the world. For, indeed, that's all who ever have."

The old saying that "behind every successful man is a great woman" doesn't pertain to my marriage. Instead of standing behind me, my wife is right next to me. We have been side by side during our entire journey. We are in this together. As we know, our businesses are often a wild roller coaster ride of emotions. Isn't it nice to have someone to talk with who props us up and renews our desires to keep moving forward? Isn't it nice to have someone who listens to our struggles, doubts, and worries? Isn't it nice to have someone who praises what we do, never demeaning our ideas or visions? My home is my sanctuary where I recharge my battery. I come home on empty and my wife is there to fill me up. My wife is directly responsible for my transition from a self-absorbed young whippersnapper to a service-minded professional.

Vickie repeatedly demonstrates how, together, we can conquer all that life throws our way by keeping our chin up, working together, trusting each other, honoring each other, being faithful in our love for each other, and, most importantly, having faith in God. She is my moral strength; she regularly reminds me to stand strong in my faith and not to be tempted by worry, as God's promise is that he has everything under control. She reminds me of what is really most important in life and that adversity is just a blip on the radar screen. Furthermore, Vickie's inner strength is remarkable to witness, and she is the most loving, caring, kind, honest, and generous person I know. I owe my success to my wife for her unwavering support and encouragement.

J.T. Townsend epitomizes perseverance and commitment like no other. He was just an ordinary young man pushed beyond his limits to confront uncertainty, fear, and pain. Growing up, J.T. had dreams of becoming a professional football player, and he was well on his way as he accepted a scholarship to play football at Florida State University. This 17-year-old, six-foot-three-inch, 180-pound strong safety's dream was cut short when he was paralyzed from the neck down in a 2004 high-school football game. "I went in to make the tackle. I hit the guy and fell to the ground. When I tried to get up, I wasn't able to get up," he said. J.T. knew something was very wrong and so did everyone around him, as he began gasping for air, went unconscious, and was rushed to the hospital.

Despite the fact that J.T. would need a wheelchair for the rest of his life, he was prepared to move forward by turning tragedy into triumph. J.T.'s spinal injury took most of his physical ability but didn't take away his burning ambition to accomplish his purpose and passion to fulfill his newly acquired dreams. Against insurmountable odds, J.T. committed to lead as normal a life as possible. While persevering through extraordinary obstacles, J.T. graduated from the University of North Florida in May 2013 with a degree in sports management. In 2011, while facing many roadblocks, physical pain, and difficulties, he established the J.T. Townsend Foundation to provide disabled children and adults with medical equipment and assistance. With his limited capacity, J.T. gave more to others than many of us who are fully functional. J.T. was extremely grateful for the tremendous support that he had received since his injury, and one of his dreams was to repay the community that had helped him when he needed help the most. J.T. simply wanted to pay it forward. He took a life-changing situation and turned it into an opportunity to make life better for those less fortunate and he gave all the glory to God. Never once did J.T. feel sorry for himself. He never asked, "Why me?'" He knew it was God's purpose.

J.T.'s life stands for inspiration, passion, courage, commitment, perseverance, service, and love for all. J.T. told me, "We must have a strong mind, believe in God, keep our faith and live every day like it's our last." This picture of J.T. and me was taken on June 2, 2013, two days before he died from a heart attack, in his home, while posting a message on his foundation's Facebook page. This incredible 26-year-old role model demonstrated just how powerful a persistent mind can be. If someone had the right to give up on his dreams and accept defeat, J.T. did. Surrendering to adversity wasn't even a consideration for J.T. Instead, he persevered and redefined defeat, not according to his physical restrictions but according to the size of his dreams.

To have been a part of J.T.'s journey has been a humbling and inspiring honor for me. The most important lessons I learned from J.T. was that one can often gain more wisdom from observing those who are less fortunate than from observing those who have more. Witnessing J.T.'s accomplishment during the past ten years underscored my conviction that if we want something badly enough, then we can get it. Nobody and nothing could prevent J.T. from choosing to be exceptional and that applies to every one of us, as well.

David Bach has enjoyed one the most remarkable success stories of anyone that I personally know. David has been a true inspiration to me for many years. I was fortunate to meet David about 17 years ago, well before his rise to stardom, while he was a successful financial advisor with Morgan Stanley. If you don't know David Bach, you may have pulled a Rip Van Winkle, as David has written multiple books on *The New York Times* bestseller list, such as *The Automatic Millionaire* and *Start Late, Finish Rich*. His latest book is titled *Debt Free for Life: The Finish Rich Plan for Financial Freedom*. In total, he has more than seven million books in print, translated into about 20 languages.

There is something very different about David that you don't see in very many people. Money is not his driving force. In its place is his passion and purpose in life. During the past two decades, I have closely watched Dave climb the ladder of success and although I am fascinated by what he has accomplished both professionally and personally, I am not surprised. David proved to me that if you absolutely believe in something, have purpose, passion, and are willing to pay the price for success, then you can accomplish your dreams.

According to an intriguing article in *Forbes* online magazine (January 16, 2012), in which Dan Schawbel interviews David Bach, when David wrote his first book, *Smart Women Finish Rich*, his mission was to educate one million women about money so that they could teach their families and kids how to be smarter with their finances. He felt this was his purpose in life, and he did not listen to the naysayers and dream killers. Instead, David had total clarity about what he intended to do. His dream began in 1994 when he found his mission and purpose in life, and he went narrow and deep. In the *Forbes* interview, David said, "The beauty of truly loving what you do is you can get through the tough times, because you feel in your soul it's your mission and purpose in life. And people can also tell when you truly love what you do versus doing something for the money."

I met Anthony Lombardi in August 2013. Similar to other significant people in my life, Tony embodies a sincere and caring demeanor, and he wants to be a difference maker. He leads with his heart while trying to become a positive influence on the way people work and live. A friend of mine, Scott Johnson, enthusiastically recommended that I spend three days with Tony to acquire knowledge about a revolutionary business model that Tony had perfected over the past 18 years. Scott explained that Tony's business approach provides proactive CPAs and tax attorneys with an in-house knowledge hub and a proprietary process of identifying and delivering optimal solutions for their most important clients while providing a world-class experience without the inherent risks that come from referring business to third parties.

After much consideration and due diligence, I took the leap of faith and followed Scott's suggestion. Devoting 72 hours to consulting Tony has been a real game-changer for me. Tony is a fearless trailblazer with remarkable enthusiasm and fervor for life, which he defines as his faith, family, and friends. Tony's passion is heart warming and contagious. After spending just a short time with Tony, it quickly became evident that he had a clear sense of purpose and vision for making a difference in people's lives.

Tony's business philosophy epitomizes the word *relationship*. Money is not his driving force. His driving force is developing meaningful relationships and doing what is right for the end user, the CPA's clients. Tony is a consummate leader and visionary with an intense hunger to take the financial service industry away from selling a product to being an authentic service model. The business model is refreshing, and it is powerful. I know words such as *life-changing* and *revolutionary* get thrown around a lot, but this is the real deal. My personal alignment with Anthony Lombardi's fundamental methodology and thought process is one of the primary reasons I wrote this book.

When I think of Vickie, J.T., David, and Tony, among other difference makers, I am reminded of the power of a positive attitude. Yes indeed, the way we think about things, our attitude, is a commanding force and how we use it could result in each one of us being a big-time difference maker. Okay folks, it is time to put on our swim caps and arm-floaties and dive into the uncharted water.

TABLE OF CONTENTS

CHAPTER 1

From Underdog to High Achiever

Before we go any further, I want to set the record straight. I am not a retired self-anointed authority or overhyped consultant who never practices what he preaches. Furthermore, I am not a self-proclaimed business guru, and I do not want to be. I am not that guy who assumes he knows everything, including the molecular structure of organic molecules and the latest and greatest investments and stock tips, all while living from paycheck to paycheck. I am not important or special. I am just an ordinary guy who works diligently, masters his subject, creates value for his clients, and serves them passionately. I have been a financial advisor since 1985, and I humbly admit I have much more to learn. I have to reaffirm my expertise every day while I walk my talk. I am on the line of fire, just like you.

I have more flaws, weaknesses, and vulnerabilities than I care to admit and a list of failures as long as my arm. My private experience with pain was horrible, but, in the end, all of it was necessary for my personal growth. When the messenger of misery pays a visit, I simply refer to this as an "ouch" moment. Of course, it hurts. It's frustrating. It's discouraging, but it is just an ouch that will eventually prove to be a valuable life lesson. I have had so many ouches that I consider myself a consummate ouchmaster. I suggest that if we were all to become ouchmasters, we would view our setbacks and adversities in a significantly different light that would ultimately illuminate the path to our success. Life has a way of dealing us cards that never seem to add up to much. Continuing to get bad cards for long enough eventually wears us down and we give up on our dream. As ouchmasters, we don't give up, because we know that the more ouches we receive, the more likely we are to reach our dream. This is not about being tough; it's about passion and belief in ourselves. Some people call me tough, akin to a Rottweiler chewing a large, juicy T-bone. I am not a tough sort of person in any sense of the word. In fact, I've only been in two fights my entire life, and my sister won both!

I am successful by industry standards because I am never willing to give up. I have run the gauntlet of highs and lows, achievements and disappointments, and my success has nothing to do with my intellect, salesmanship, or whether anyone sees me as some type of guru. I experienced failure and adversity at a very deep level throughout my career as a financial advisor. I simply ouched my way to the top. Struggles are a beautiful thing and I carry all my black-and-blues very proudly. My struggles are a big part of my story and I would not trade any of them, because they made me who I am. In the end, I simply chose the pain of discipline over the pain of regret.

Of course, none of us are strangers to the pain of struggle. Isn't part of the excitement of reaching our goals looking back at all the obstacles we overcame and the pain we endured? Don't our struggles make the victory that much more satisfying and rewarding? At some point in our lives, we eventually realize that adversity is a valuable part of life, as it is through our pain and suffering that we develop the mental capacity to endure the toughest battles.

While I have never been the sharpest knife in the drawer, I have been told numerous times that I am a perfectionist and intensely curious. I am obsessed with personal growth. I am addicted to productivity because, in my view, there is a short distance between the penthouse and the outhouse. Regrettably, I am so wired for quality and excellence that I tend to be cynical. I am not a very patient person and I have a strong and stubborn conviction on many issues.

I am not content with resting on my laurels, as I am emotionally and intellectually committed to continually searching for methods to accomplish things more professionally, more cost effectively, and more efficiently. I consider my business to be an engine that I fine-tune every day. My machine operates efficiently. It runs with passion. It is dependable. It is fruitful, but most importantly, my engine has a heart! I am especially interested in developing systems and discovering methods to empower people to collaborate more proficiently to deliver their goals. I believe one of the primary reasons for business failure is the lack of systems. Time and again in small businesses, the owner is the system. Everything is accomplished based on the owner's instincts. I believe that if people cannot define what they do as a process, then they don't know what they are doing. Without efficient systems that successfully automate processes, it is virtually impossible to sustain a business for the long run.

Practically everything that I perform in my business, I have acquired from someone else. I seldom try to reinvent the wheel. I simply model success. I learn from people much smarter and more successful than I am—people who have accomplished what I am trying to achieve. Among the hundreds of books I have devoured, one stands head and shoulders above them all: the book of Proverbs. It has more application, common sense, and wisdom than anything else in my library. Proverbs is about discipline and relationships and how to improve both. What I am about to share with you embodies both.

I believe so strongly in the book of Proverbs and its ability to empower you to succeed in business and your personal life that I have scattered a few of my favorite proverbs throughout these pages. If you are not familiar with the book of Proverbs, it is the second book of the third section of the Hebrew Bible. Solomon was born around 974 BC and became king of Israel at the incredibly young age of 12. Solomon was frightened by his enormous responsibilities. According to the Old Testament, God spoke to him, asking what he required as the new king of Israel. To God's surprise, Solomon asked only for wisdom and guidance so that he could effectively lead the people of Israel. God was so impressed with Solomon's answer that he provided him with more wisdom, knowledge, riches, wealth, and honor than anyone.

I can imagine what you might be thinking right now: "Hey, I am not a Bible reader, don't care about Mr. Solomon, and I don't want some guy evangelizing to me." I get it. Over and out! Frankly, I am especially sensitive to discussing politics and religion with just about everyone except my wife and children. Nevertheless, my intentions are for the best: I hope that you will benefit as much as I have from applying this gold mine of divine wisdom.

While I argue that knowledge and wisdom are paramount to success, they have virtually no meaning if no action is taken to employ them. Knowledge is only potential power and only becomes legitimate power when used in a systematized fashion to accomplish goals. What good is it to read, understand, and agree with Solomon's insight if we don't apply his wisdom to our business and personal lives? As someone once told me, "I don't care if you know it; I care how good you are at it." This is not a knowledge book. Knowledge is simply the acquiring of information. This is an action book. I am not hawking information; I am offering you a dream to the better way, a better life. I want you to get it, absorb it, believe it, and be inspired and influenced by it. "The great aim of education," said Herbert Spencer, "is not knowledge but action."

> Knowledge is only potential power and only becomes legitimate power when used in a systematized fashion to accomplish one's goals.

The true value of this book is not what I write, but what you take out of your reading and apply to your business and life. I want my words to connect with you, to inspire and motivate you to take action, as good intentions and a positive outlook are rarely enough. Knowledge and intentions mean nothing. What matters most is that you take action. Most people don't fail because of their many mistakes; they fail because they never chose to act.

Anyone can obtain knowledge, which is why I believe college diplomas are not as big a deal as they were back in the day. Indeed, I submit that knowledge in itself isn't worth very much. If you don't agree, check out the payroll of any university or college. Ultimately, the power of this book rests in its application.

Proverbs 15:31—If you listen to correction to improve your life, you will live among the wise.

TURNING POINT–NOT BY A LONG SHOT

Think about a time in your life when you can say your life changed for the better. This is the turning point: a time in our lives when we initiated change. Most people have turning points in their lives. My first major turning point happened in 1985 when I was a miserable, conflicted 25-year-old misfit, flying the friendly skies as a flight attendant for a major airline. Yep, I was one of the "steward-esses," as some old timers like to call them. For two and a half years I felt that I was walking in my sleep and going through the motions, while I served soft drinks and peanuts and lived with a couple of roommates named Mom and Dad. I was stuck in neutral and com-pletely unhappy but did not have a clue what I wanted to accom-plish in life. There was no purpose, no passion, no desire—nothing! I knew I wanted something better, but perhaps I was waiting for that something to magically happen. My life was like a mystery and I was the main character trying to solve the puzzle. Then it happened. Bam! The aha! moment.

I found my breakthrough, my epiphany, my Eureka moment, as if a bright light were unexpectedly turned on for me. The idea flashed in my head. I immedi-ately saw things in a completely different fashion. There I was at 30,000 feet delivering a coke and peanuts to a well-dressed businessman, when all of a sudden, everything was moving in slow motion. That was it, no more waiting for things to

"I think I just had an epiphany. How do I make it go away?"

24

magically appear. It was time. No one was coming to save me, so I made a choice for myself. I discovered my inner power. I was no longer going to let chance direct my life. Instead, I was going to take control of my destiny. I was no longer going to blame others or circumstances for my life. I was going to take control. I was going from victim to victor.

While having dinner that evening with my wife (fiancée at that time), I said, "Vickie, I'm quitting! I am turning in my wings. I want to do more with my life and career. I am going to be a financial advisor and make a difference in people's lives and if I can do that, the money will follow. Remaining a flight attendant won't serve that purpose."

After a few days of procrastination, I took the plunge. I was ready but terribly frightened! I polished my shoes, waxed my '81 used gold Camaro, put on my only suit, and I was off to downtown Pittsburgh, Pennsylvania, intent on becoming a rising star in the financial service business. Whoa! I was in for a rude awakening. Just about every brokerage firm door was slammed in my face after I was politely told, "If we are interested, we will call you." The repeated rejections were brutal. Nobody believed in me, except for my fiancée. Although I was a naïve 25-year-old kid, who looked 16, with a resume that showed no selling experience, and my only previous occupation was that of a flight attendant, I wasn't giving up! I was determined, with staunch conviction, to be the long shot that won the race! My award would be to put a thumb in the eye of all the naysayers.

> Most people don't fail because of their many mistakes; they fail because they never chose to act.

Call it bottom dog, slim chance, no chance, one in a million, dud, or hundred to one, the truth of the matter is I was a long shot, or, according to my many critics, hopelessly beyond consideration. I was devastated, but the underdog title was never a problem for me. I was accustomed to it. Bring it on! I accepted the challenge. There was no retreat in me. I just attacked in a different direction

I didn't know this at the time, but I began doing something that proved to be directly attributed to my success: I kept asking and asking and asking. My perseverance and belief in myself was unwavering. I had the commitment to see my vision through. Nothing was going to stop me. Nothing! After a boatload of rejections, relentless phone calls, visits, and letters to managers of every brokerage office in Pittsburgh, I finally made a score. I remember it as if it were yesterday when I got a call from a representative at a local branch who invited me to meet with the branch manager. While I nervously waited in the lobby for my scheduled interview, an impeccably dressed stocky gentleman, who stood about five foot seven inches and had a well-groomed comb-over, introduced himself as the branch manager. At the end of our surprisingly short meeting, Joe (his real name) invited me to take two standard tests, which supposedly measured a candidate's future success as a financial advisor. After about two weeks, Joe called me back into his office to discuss the results. I was pumped as I told my wife, "I must have nailed the tests. Joe wouldn't make me drive 30 minutes back into downtown Pittsburgh just to tell me that I had bombed."

After a few words of chit chat, Joe eyeballed me with a stern look and said, "Harry, I have bad news and some good news." I immediately thought I must have done well on one test and not the other. Nevertheless, Joe glared at me in his unique and intimidating manner and said, "Harry, you flunked the aptitude test. This is the test that tells us how likely you are to pass the required licensing test to become a financial advisor." I quickly replied, "How did I do on the other?" He grinned and said, "You performed worse!" I thought, "You jerk. You are smiling at me while you insinuate that I am a bust!" Joe went on to say, "Harry, the second test measures your sales acumen and the results tell us that your success is highly unlikely as a financial advisor." I was stunned. Tears began to fill my eyes. I gave Joe a stern look and belted out, "Joe, forget these exams. A true test judges a person on results. I will learn what is necessary to become a thriving financial advisor, because I have the passion and commitment to be the best. You can teach anyone how to sell, but you can't teach anyone to work as I will. Give me the job, Joe." To my surprise, Joe said, "That's the good news, Harry. There is something special about you, and I am willing to take a chance that others advise me not to take." Fast forward a few months and it was a heart-warming and proud day for Joe and me when the firm presented me with a certificate in honor of being the most valuable rookie (MVR) in my training class.

I started my job with plenty of enthusiasm, conviction, and passion, but little else. I had no sales experience and no contacts. My resources were limited, but my willingness to work was unlimited. I had something to prove to Joe, myself, and everyone else who didn't believe in me. I put the blinders on for the next five years while I dialed for dollars, six days a week, every week, for five years! I had no other option. I decided to be another cold-call cowboy! I heard the word "No" so many times that it absolutely had zero impact on me. In fact, I wanted to hear "No," because the more I heard it, the closer I was to yes. I am proud to say that I was always among the leaders in opening new accounts. No magic. I just out-dialed everyone else. Fast-forward to today and here I am writing my second book, sharing my secrets to success. People familiar with my success often say I have a Midas touch, or that I have just been lucky. If people only knew how hard I worked and the price I paid to master my profession, they wouldn't think I am so special! I certainly don't have a Midas touch and "luck" is all about great planning and careful execution. I have flourished because I have a burning desire to succeed and I care immensely about my clients. It is amazing how simple it is to succeed when you genuinely care about your clients!

Of all the discoveries I have made during my career, the most important was the need for sacrifice. The underachievers tend to follow the path of least resistance. To put it differently, they want to get as much as possible with the least amount of effort. Vince Lombardi may have said it best, "The dictionary is the only place where success comes before work." Hard work is the price we pay for success. We can accomplish almost anything if we are willing to pay the price.

"All of my professors told us the key to success is doing something you love. I love living at home with you and mom."

Sadly, most folks won't cowboy up when times get tough. Instead, they do whatever they can to avoid pain, failure, and adversity, because that is how we are programmed. Unfortunately, most folks don't use their failures as stepping-stones to bigger and better things. Instead, they become fearful and question their beliefs, which ultimately holds them back from achieving their life's ambition. The ability to persist through adversity is what separates the achievers from the sustainers. We all know that we will fail multiple times in life. That much is guaranteed. What is not guaranteed is how we will react to adversity. Most people won't fight through the frustration and pain. It is easier to wave the white flag and surrender. This reminds me of the February 10, 1962, fight between 20-year-old Muhammad Ali (Cassius Clay at the time) and Sunny Banks. Ali was undefeated, with a record of 10-0, and he was coming off his Olympic gold medal. Bam! A powerful left hook to the body and down went Ali for the first time in his career. As the referee started his count, Ali quickly sat up and told himself this was not the position of a champion. He jumped to his feet and proceeded to hit Mr. Banks so hard that Mrs. Banks got a headache! Not only did the Champ get up from the canvas in the first round, but he also knocked out Banks three rounds later, just as he predicted! This wonderful example proves the point that it is not about how many times we hit the canvas; it's about our willingness to get up and continue to fight. Ali went on to become the World Heavyweight Champion two years later, in 1964.

Of course, this trek is not for everyone, as it requires the faith to break through the usual human hang-ups regarding change. When we mix faith with an idea and use our imagination, we are on our way to successville! Then we add lots of purpose and passion, oh my! Then we top that off with a detailed step-by-step systematic plan to fulfill our dream and bingo! We did it. We tried something different and knocked it out of the park. Nothing was going to stop us from reaching our dreams, not even the fear of change! Regrettably, most people don't embrace change. They read and absorb material but won't apply what they learned. The folks who do apply what they learn normally give up when circumstances become too difficult. They hear the familiar inner voice that whispers, "Please, no more. I can't take any more pain." This is when the white flag is raised in surrender and the dreams are lost.

In fact, just about everybody will do what is necessary to resist making changes because of the potential pain that they may encounter. I am reminded of the story about an elderly man who was celebrating his birthday. A newspaper reporter covering the story said to the elderly gentleman, "Sir, you must have seen a great many changes during the past 100 years." The old man looked at the reporter, snarled, and said, "Yes, and I have been against every one of them!"

Different from the old man, you will have to step out of your comfort zone of tax preparation into a different world of financial advisory services and embrace the change and opportunity presented to you. While knowledge is imperative, you attain nothing without action. Success comes to the forward-thinking and humble professional who is willing to be influenced by another professional. I know it won't be easy, but I plan to do whatever I can to become a positive influence in your life. I am ready for the challenge. Are you?

Proverbs 24:10—If you falter in times of trouble,
how small is your strength!

To prosper and make a difference in our professions, we must be in a state of constant change. I operate under the constant and never-ending improvement (CANI) philosophy. I regularly imagine what could be, and I am not afraid to take action. I consider Albert Einstein's quote to be spot on: "Imagination is more important than knowledge!"

I am not a man of great intellect. Fortunately, my business does not require abundant brainpower. What it does require is a burning desire to be the best. In my observation of thriving people, it is perfectly clear that achievement does not necessarily come to those with the highest IQ, or those who went to the best colleges, or even those who chose the most sought-after degree. Instead, lifelong drive and determination are better predictors of professional and personal success.

I am adamant that the way of success is the continuous pursuit of applied knowledge. One of my favorite quotes is from Mahatma Gandhi: "Live as if you were to die tomorrow. Learn as if you were to live forever." I have read more than 500 professional and personal development books. During the past 28 years, I have been a sponge soaking up anything with the words "how to" in it. I often have been told that I ask too many questions, but I feel that every person I meet knows something more than I do. I want to know what it is and see whether I can apply it to my personal and business life. I know what I know, and now I want to know what you know. So I enter every situation asking questions instead of giving answers. Learning doesn't stop when we get a college diploma. That is when real learning begins.

CHAPTER 2

Why I Wrote This Book: The Aha! Moment

Before I jump into the details, let me explain, simply and clearly, the four primary reasons why I wrote this book:

- **Inspire:** I want to be a great example for someone to emulate, an ordinary guy who overcame many obstacles to reach a level of success that is admirable. Having the wherewithal to empower another individual is a precious gift that should be used.

- **Influence:** I want to be a difference maker. I want people to learn from me so they can improve their lives and achieve their goals.
- **Imprint:** I want to make a long-lasting impact in the accounting and wealth-management profession.
- **Income:** If I am able to inspire and influence people to take successful action, money will follow, which will allow me the opportunity to continue my purpose and passion.

Can you remember a moment when a brilliant idea flashed into your head? It is that epiphany, that aha! moment when you begin to see things in a completely different fashion. Some people refer to this experience as a paradigm shift, as if a bright light were suddenly turned on.

I had another major aha! moment while reading a February 21, 2013, article by Brian Hartstein titled "CPAs as a Center of Influence: The New Paradigm." The article described the dramatic shift taking place in the accounting profession as forward-thinking CPA firms embrace a new approach to serving their best clients. The author suggests that CPAs will no longer refer business to outside professional advisors. Instead, everything is being kept "in-house," where a designated financial advisor is backed by a team of experts in a variety of areas, ranging from specialized qualified and nonqualified planning to asset management and protection. The CPA is afforded full access to the "knowledge hub," with the advisor acting as information manager of the hub. Nothing is presented to the CPA's client without the CPA's direct involvement. In the final analysis, this unique business methodology solves a distinct, immediate, and ongoing problem that is taking place in the accounting and wealth-management profession: how to integrate wealth-management services into a CPA practice. Moreover, this innovative approach is easy to access, understand, and implement. More importantly, it gets fast proven results.

This is a time in the economy when people are looking for advice. Enormous numbers of people are struggling, trying to figure out how to accomplish things. They want and need help to get them from where they are to where they want to be. They are looking for experts who have been there and done that and who can provide them with the blueprint to success. The biggest stumbling block is trust, not money. People need to fully trust the "guru" and believe that there is value in what is being offered. I faithfully believe I can be that expert. I have figured out the path, and I get things done. Period! When I truly believe in something, I feel the need to share my message, and I write and speak about it with great confidence, professionalism, and enthusiasm.

Many people who write and speak first determine what the audience wants and then adjust their message to match the needs. I am not a hack who panders to masses. My message is not about what I imagine my audience wants to hear. I am not a manipulator seeking to influence people to do something that I wouldn't do. Rather, I seek out people who want to hear my story. I write from my heart about a message that I believe will empower CPAs and financial advisors to take their personal and professional lives to a level they never imagined. I have a passion to share my message, even if it touches the heart and mind of just one person.

"You are truly a great man," a hotel guest once told the Christian evangelist Billy Graham as they rode an elevator. "No, I am not a great man," Graham replied. "I just have a great message." Of course, my message pales in comparison, but my enthusiasm and conviction are just as pronounced.

My words at times may seem overconfident or pompous, which is certainly not my intent, but I am steadfastly dedicated to my profession and beliefs, and I want to share what I have found incredibly exciting. Furthermore, in the pages ahead, if I fail to be eloquent, please understand that I write to be understood. I want my readers to "get it," which is why I am going after your heart as well as your mind. I know that my written words lack much of the passion and electricity that I display when speaking to a large audience. Nevertheless, much of what you will read, I wrote as if I were delivering a keynote address.

There are words other than *eloquent* that describe me: energy, passion, conviction, enthusiasm, confidence, spot on, real world, and so on. Also, my writing and speaking does not recognize gender, so please don't get hung up on my use of the word *his*. It is not my intention to insult the many successful women in accounting and financial services. I am simply trying to express my message with compassion, clarity, and confidence in order to help you understand and to enable you to seize the golden opportunity in front of you.

I wrote this book with the CPA in mind. However, there is tremendous application for financial advisors. I only wish I had been able to read something like this when I started in the business. It truly would have been a game changer.

I understand what it took for you to buy this book and I have incredible respect for you because you have invested your time and money in this reading. Moreover, I deeply admire the fact that you are bringing your dreams into the daylight to seek a better way, a better life. That's why I have such a high opinion of you. I am sure you want to make things happen, but you are disappointed with the way the ideas that inspired you panned out. I feel for you because I too have struggled with the same problem. I am quite confident that if you follow the framework that I provide, good things will come your way. You have taken the biggest step by purchasing this book. Now it's time to get focused, have some fun, and make it happen.

Of course, you may decide that change is not necessary. In fact, Warren Buffett said that there are situations where patching the leaks is much easier and more productive than getting into a new boat. In the end, you are the one who needs to ask yourself the tough question that requires a heart-felt and truthful answer: "Is there really a need for change?" If so, when is change necessary? Regardless of your decision, I am quite confident that what you gain from reading this book will help you to decide if adjustments are necessary for your business and personal life so that you can become more prosperous.

Be confident that throughout this book I recommend nothing dishonest or immoral. In truth, those who know me understand that I can handle just about anything except a lie. I simply cannot tolerate lying to take advantage of someone. Honesty is important to me and I hold my staff, friends, and family to the same high standards. I built a reputation on the foundation of trust and integrity and consistent truth. Conducting one's business and personal life any other way produces never-ending stress.

This book will deliver my message in a simple, honest, and truthful fashion. I will not distort facts or spin the truth. I will call things what they are, in the manner of Buffett, who is known for his no-nonsense straight talk. He means what he says and says what he means. The Corn-Fed Capitalist doesn't put lipstick on a pig. He straight out calls a pig a pig. He shares the truth, which is why every year, with great anticipation, investors look forward to reading the Forrest Gump of finance's management letter in his company's annual report. The audience gets the facts with no spin. Those who are trusted are candid and not afraid to tell the truth even if it sheds a poor light on them. They simply share the truth, and that is what I will do for you. Everything rests on credibility. Nothing destroys believability more quickly than spinning your story into make-believe land. A wise man once told me that no wealth or success can endure unless it is built on truth and ethics.

Proverbs 10:9—Whoever walks in integrity walks securely, but whoever takes crooked paths will be found out.

In preparation for this book, I meticulously studied, read, listened to, and watched everything and anything that dealt with the issue in question. I was on a quest to learn, internalize, and synthesize as much information as possible in the shortest time. I wanted to know everything about the accounting profession as it relates to incorporating a wealth-management service in general, and this intriguing, unique and cutting-edge business model in particular. My mission has been an all-consuming challenge. Although it has been expensive, stressful, frustrating, and lonely, I reminded myself that my message will make a difference in people's lives. Of course, you will be the one who decides that.

Nonetheless, it was crucial for me to stay connected to why I was writing this book, because that is what kept me going. I have applied the same principles to this undertaking as I have with my wealth advisory practice as well as my personal life: work diligently, master my subject, create value for my clients, and serve them passionately. In the end, I have laid my heart out on these pages and I believe from the depths of my soul that my efforts in completing this book will be worth all the headaches, sleepless nights, and temporary defeats that I have experienced on my odyssey.

Proverbs 24:5-6—The wise are mightier than the strong, and those with knowledge grow stronger and stronger. So don't go to war without wise guidance; victory depends on having many advisers.

My primary objective in writing this book is to persuade you to take action. I will try my best to present my point of view in a clear and compelling way to motivate you to do what I believe to be in your best interest. We are now at point A and I want to get you to point B. At the moment, you know little about me and my business. You may be skeptical, resistant, and, maybe, already committed to a position contrary to what I am recommending. If I have any chance of moving you to point B, everything that I say and suggest must serve your needs, not mine. In fact, the following questions were always on my mind when I was putting my pen to paper:

1. Does this idea solve a real problem for my reader?
2. Why is this important to my reader?
3. What does this mean to my reader?
4. Why am I telling my reader this?
5. Why should my reader care?
6. How does my reader benefit?
7. Does this idea help my reader achieve market distinction?
8. Is the idea user friendly?
9. Will this idea produce enthusiasm in my reader?

Furthermore, I will do my best to help you to understand, believe, and, most importantly, act. All three undertakings are critical. If you don't understand, you won't believe and then, of course, you won't act. Neither does understanding guarantee that you will believe, and getting you to act could be the biggest challenge. I understand that you arrive at your own stage of readiness to move forward in your own time. You have your own agenda, wants, and desires. Perhaps you are stressed out, occupied, and feel that there is simply not enough time to get things accomplished. Furthermore, my strong hunch is that most professionals, and CPAs in particular, are highly resistant to anyone making suggestions about how they should conduct their business.

WIIFY

What's in it for you (WIIFY)? Most people most of the time are not motivated to do what you want them to do. They want to help themselves and their family. I get it. It is human nature. I am the same way. Don't provide me with a long list of all your features. Don't provide me with the sizzle and no steak. Where's the beef? I want benefits! In other words, how can what you have to offer serve me?

I hear you. I know that it isn't about getting what I want. It is all about providing you with what you want. With that clear, let's move on to the five primary benefits to you by employing this innovative business concept: The Better Way.

1. It will empower you to become irreplaceable in the eyes of your most important clients.
2. It will increase your revenues and overall value beyond tax season by incorporating financial services into your practice.
3. It will provide you with a collection of turnkey best-practice strategies for business acquisition and client retention.
4. You can complete more while working less so that you will have more time to enjoy the things that are most important to you.

5. No capital or obligation is required from you.

Furthermore, The Better Way will save you time and money.

I refer to the above as my IVP (irresistible value proposition). If someone approached me with the aforementioned business objectives, that person would get my attention. While I would be skeptical, I would say, "Sign me up." You are probably thinking, "Oh, puh-lease! Do you expect me to believe that you intend to help me accomplish all of the above without any cost to me or obligation on my part?" Yes, of course, and why not? Let me explain further in story form:

A VALUABLE BUSINESS LESSON FROM NATURE

In nature, bees and flowers each have their respective needs. Bees make their living from the flowers by gathering nectar and turning it into honey. Flowers require the bees for pollination in order to grow. In the nature of our business, we are the bees buzzing around with excitement from flower to flower in order to get what we need.

Since there are only limited numbers of "flowers," bees consume a lot of energy traveling long distances to satisfy their needs. During their travels, they regularly find other bees competing for the nectar, causing them to work harder to get what they need. Eventually, the bees' wings get too tired to continue the fight for nectar, resulting in their demise.

If we don't give, we don't get!

In all of this buzzing excitement, the flower remains still, while laughing at the enthusiastic bees. The flower is clever. It understands that it produces such great content (nectar) that it draws the bees in. The flower stays grounded and uses all its time and resources to keep producing newer, sweeter content (nectar). The bees can't resist the value of the flower and the buzzing excitement starts all over again. The flower gets pollinated and multiplies throughout the fields. The flower's only concern is how to appeal to the bees. If the flowers do this, the bees will continue to seek them out.

I hope you connect with the moral of the story: if we don't give, we don't get! Additionally, we should accept that we must implement a business strategy that produces exceptional value to our clients (bees) so they seek us out and return again and again. That's what I intend to do for you.

LESS PRODUCES MORE

I have learned that great business ideas, life's lessons, and wisdom can come from anywhere or anyone, such as a book, article, mentors, family, conferences, and even a movie. Do you remember the 1996 box office hit Jerry Maguire? This engaging film spoke to me in numerous ways. It was as if the script had been written with this book in mind. You probably remember the movie's famous line, "Show me the money!" It's one of the best movie moments in recent memory. But money is not what I want to talk about. In its place, I would like to address the film's message about the importance of relationships. Tom Cruise is Jerry Maguire, a high-powered professional sports agent who has so many clients that it becomes difficult for him to express how much he really cares about them. In the midst of a sleepless night, Jerry has an epiphany. Disgusted by his life as a "shark in a suit," Jerry writes a memo (mission statement) that he distributes to all of his associates,

42

encouraging them to follow a simple principle: "Fewer clients, less money, more personal attention." Jerry calls on himself and his colleagues to think more about the long-term interests of their clients and less about making money. Jerry's superiors think his ideas are unhealthy for business, and he promptly loses his job. His fall from grace motivates him to put his new philosophy to the test as an independent sports agent with the help of one loyal colleague and one outrageous client, Rod Tidwell (Cuba Gooding Jr.). Jerry Maguire learns that loving well is the best revenge. Here is an excerpt from Jerry's aha! moment.

> Who had I become? Just another shark in a suit? Two days later, at our corporate conference in Miami, a breakthrough. Breakdown? Breakthrough. I couldn't escape one simple thought. I hated myself ... no, no, no. Here's what it was: I hated my place ... in the world. I had so much to say and no one to listen, and then it happened. It was the oddest, most unexpected thing. I began writing what they call a mission statement, not a memo, a mission statement, you know, a suggestion for the future of our company. A night like this doesn't come along very often. I seized it. What started out as one page became twenty-five. Suddenly, I was my father's son again. I was remembering the simple pleasures of this job, how I ended up here out of law school, the way a stadium sounds when one of my players performs well on the field ... the way we are meant to protect them in health and in injury. With so many clients, we had forgotten what was important. I wrote and wrote and wrote and wrote ... and I'm not even a writer. I was remem-

bering the words of the original sports agent, my mentor, the late great Dickey Fox, who said, "The key to this business is personal relationships." And suddenly it was all pretty clear. The answer was fewer clients. Less money. More attention, caring for them, caring for ourselves, and games too. Just starting our lives, really! Hey, I'll be the first to admit that what I was writing was somewhat touchy feely. I didn't care. I had lost the ability to b--- s---. It was the me I had always wanted to be. I took it in a bag to a Copymat in the middle of the night and printed 110 copies. Even the cover looked like The Catcher in the Rye ... I entitled it The Things We Think and Do Not Say: The Future of Our Business

Proverbs 11:2—When pride comes, so does shame,
but wisdom brings humility.

LESSONS FROM *JERRY MCGUIRE*

- **Connect:** Connect with our clients on a personal level. Fewer clients and more personal relationships is a better strategy.
- **Care:** Lead with the heart! When our relationships are overflowing with genuine care, magical things happen.
- **Contribute:** Givers gain! It's about giving first and then receiving.
- **Courage:** Willing to lose it all in order to find peace in what we do.

- **Charisma:** Being skilled communicators is paramount if we want to be persons of influence.

In the end, Jerry's point is clear. To be successful in our business, the focus should not be on how many clients we have, but on the strength of our relationships and quality of service. Better service and loyal clients emerge and then the money follows. This memorable romantic comedy is all about the courage to change. As most of us know, it is always difficult to part ways with the old and experience the new. Even when we acknowledge that change is necessary, we are still creatures of habit. Jerry is different. He recognizes that his time has arrived. He has to change. Jerry and his client uncover the meaning of loyalty and learn to value something far more significant than money. They realize that money can't be a substitute for a burning desire to see a vision to completion. Likewise, they understand that life's greatest lessons are gained from losses, if the losses are approached in the right way. They also realize that it is acceptable to be humble and not concerned with who is right. As author and business consultant, Ken Blanchard says, "Humility does not mean you think less of yourself; it means you think of yourself less."

I acknowledge that most people who read this book will not follow my advice or, for that matter, agree with much of what I have to say. Frankly, what you think of me and my message doesn't change my belief. My primary purpose is to change yours. I say this not to appear condescending, but because countless studies have concluded that precious few people actually employ what they read or hear. Additionally, studies have shown that about 95 percent of people are imitators and only 5 percent are initiators. I suggest that we must stop following the crowd if we sincerely want to accomplish something exceptional. Let's swim upstream. Let's go the other way. Let's ignore the conventional wisdom. If everybody else is doing something a certain way, then there is an excellent chance that we can find our niche by looking at the situation from a different vantage point. If we are truly attempting to make a difference, then the status quo is the enemy. We need to convey something different and exciting to the market.

" I need you to be more decisive when agreeing with me. "

Let's become the visionaries, the 5 percent who are passionate about something and go for it regardless of whether others have completed it before them. Benjamin Franklin said, "If everyone is thinking alike, then no one is thinking." In the end, business and life are not about doing more; they are about doing less and getting better results.

A word of warning: If you are searching for a fast approach that requires little discipline or hard work to help take your business to the next level, you can call off the posse right now! The myth of the overnight success happens only with lottery winners. There is no magic bullet or quick fix to reach success, and this book is not about to try. Being the best is never easy and it takes time, sacrifice, and per-severance. Nothing extraordinary is ever achieved through ordinary means. If you are looking for motivation, inspiration, direction, and a proven system that creates enormous value for your clients and at the same time provides you with more time to enjoy the things that matter most to you, then you are in the right place at the right time. This may indeed be the most important and life-changing step you make in your business.

I want to lead you into an exciting new world. There you go again with, *"Pul-lease!"* Furthermore, I can hear you uttering John McEnroe's famous meltdown quote, "You can't be serious." Make no mistake; I am dead serious. I understand that it is human nature to expect that anyone who tries to influence others has something to gain. What I don't understand or agree with is that influence means one person gains while another loses. Sure, I may benefit if you act on what you read, but if you do, three people will walk away satisfied.

> Being the best is never easy and it takes time, sacrifice, and perseverance.

I imagine that, at some point, you will feel specific parts of the reading are too soft, rah-rah, or motivational. I totally get it. I've been there, done that, and got the T-shirt. Many times, I wished the author or speaker would move it along, but in the end, I realized how all the dots were, eventually, connected. I profoundly believe that even if I have all the milk in the world, if you don't have an Oreo cookie, much of this doesn't matter. In other words, if we are not willing to pay the price for a worthy prize, then all bets are off. It has as much to do with our beliefs, passion, and commitment as it does with the business model itself. We must look at the total package. That is why I feel it is paramount that I take the time to really engage with you, heart to heart. We need to have the right mindset if we want to take the journey of a better way and a better life. So trust in the process. It will serve you and I am confident that it will put you on the fast track to success.

As part of my genuine desire to really connect with you, I have woven short stories throughout the reading. My intent is not necessarily to entertain or motivate you, though these things often happen. I find stories to be a powerful vehicle to unite an idea with an emotion, in order to make us truly feel the message. It's been proven repeatedly that stories have more effect than do lists of facts and figures, spreadsheets, and so on. When we hear or read a captivating story, we find that we have an emotional attachment to it, which normally lasts a long time. I truly hope that my "Once upon a time …" stories pull you in and empower you to consider things at a deeper level and with more clarity.

It may be tempting to read this book out of sequence, selecting the chapters that pique your interest the most. Nonetheless, I hope you will read it the way it was intended, the old fashioned way, from cover to cover, beginning to end. As you turn the final pages, it would give me much pleasure to know that you believe you spent your time and money wisely and that the book's contents are thought provoking, action oriented, and empowering. I hope my genuine concern is evident in my determination to help you as you pursue your life's goals and ambitions.

It is my desire that we disagree on only one thing: after reading the book, you will hope your competitors never read it, but I hope they do! If you are prepared to embark on this excursion with me, grab a soda, fasten your seat belt, and let's take a road trip. I will supply the inspiration, motivation, and necessary information, methods, and ideas to empower you to take your practice to the next level. In return, all I ask is that you provide the commitment to the process and desire to see it through. Fair enough?

CHAPTER 3

My Motives, Values, Experience

"I struggled for years to understand what motivates me to do the things I do. Only took the jury five minutes."

Although this book is about a highly successful business system that Tony Lombardi pioneered, it is much more than that. In fact, I can argue that it may not even be the most important message in the book. Nevertheless, rarely has my skeptical and cynical nature disappointed me. Thus, if I were in your position, reading this book for the first time, I would want to know whether the author honestly understood my needs. I would ask about the author's motives, core values, and experience. Can the author do what he claims? How much will all this cost me? I would want to feel comfortable knowing that the author had my best interest in mind and not some self-serving agenda. Let's take a look at each of these questions:

1. **Do you correctly understand what I need?** Show me that you have done your homework. Prove to me that you truly understand my issues and concerns as a CPA.

2. **What is your motive?** As Mahatma Gandhi so cleverly stated, "The moment there is suspicion about a person's motives, everything he does becomes tainted." Are you committed to my success or are you concerned more about your own achievements? If I can't trust you, nothing else really counts. If I suspect that you are a taker and not a giver, what you say in this book will have little value to me. Either you are really interested in me, and have a sincere desire to help me, or you're just trying to satisfy your own agenda.

3. **What are your core values?** We must share similar philosophies about serving clients and growing one's business. I will listen and follow someone's advice if I know that person cares deeply about making a difference. In other words, is money your driving force, or is it accomplishing something more meaningful? If it is all about the money, especially at my expense, I am not interested.

4. **Can you do what you claim?** Very few things trouble me as much as what I call the "hype of hypocrisy." Stated more simply, do you practice what you preach? As a

financial advisor, do you invest your money one way, but recommend clients do something different? I don't want to learn that you drive Fords but sell Chevys! I suspect that many authors of self-help books don't follow their own advice. What they teach doesn't work, but selling it does. They are selling the hype of hypocrisy! In addition, I get extremely annoyed with people who don't deliver on their promise. Talk is cheap! Actions speak louder than words. You need to convince me that you put to use what you are suggesting. As long as I know you have skin in the game, then I am much more likely to believe your rhetoric.

5. **What is this going to cost me?** I want full transparency. I don't like surprises, especially when it pertains to my money.

6. **What is your experience?** I want to know your experience as a so-called authority. Do you have the professional experience and expertise required to address my needs and challenges? I want to follow someone who has been there and done that. To phrase it another way: Please don't preach what you haven't practiced.

Proverbs: 21:2—All a man's ways seem right to him,
but the Lord evaluates the motives.

I would like to address the last question right now: What is your experience? I have always worked on the premise that "if you haven't done it, they won't listen to you." People listen to people who have been there and done that. However, best-selling author Brendon Burchard convinced me otherwise. He says there are two ways to become an expert. You can be a "results expert" or a "research expert."

I am considered, by most people, a results expert in my wealth-management practice. In other words, I have been there and done that and have become successful, by industry standards. However, I am considered, primarily, a research expert regarding the innovative business system that I will be discussing, as I am just beginning the journey down the road of being there and doing that. Burchard argues that a research expert is just as valuable as a results expert.

Here are two examples that illustrate my point. If you were considering buying a few rental properties as an investment, would you seek the advice of someone who has no experience in purchasing real estate? I suspect you would take a pass. Let's assume this person who lacks experience in buying and selling rental property has spent a significant amount of time interviewing some of the most profitable, forward-thinking, and experienced real estate investors in the country. Based on the valuable data he obtained, this person then created a step-by-step written process revealing how regular folks could be just as fruitful as real estate gurus. Would you have a different mindset? It is worth remembering that experts are students first.

Here is a real-life illustration: Napoleon Hill's 1937 personal-development, self-help book *Think and Grow Rich* has been called the "granddaddy of all motivational literature" and is considered the first book to confidently explain what makes a winner. Hill, as a journalist, was given an assignment to compose a series of success stories of famous men. Hill was scheduled to have a short interview with steel magnate Andrew Carnegie. This "brief" interview lasted three days, and Carnegie challenged him to interview some of the most prominent people in the world and then to develop a philosophy of success, which Hill would teach to others. Carnegie's introduction put the young Hill in contact with people who included Thomas Edison, Alexander Graham Bell, Henry Ford, Theodore Roosevelt,

William Wrigley, George Eastman, John D. Rockefeller, and F. W. Woolworth. Hill's study of their principles of success took 20 years with over 500 interviews before he wrote his first book. The legendary author simply synthesized his discussions with these successful men to develop lessons and best practices. Hill's project on the principles of success gained him the reputation for being one of the world's foremost experts on self-development. What I find fascinating is that despite the fact that Hill is considered to have helped more people become successful than any other person in history, he was never considered successful or wealthy prior to publishing his famous book. Hill was a research expert, while Carnegie, Rockefeller, Ford, and others were results experts.

As an active learner, I am excited about continuing to develop my "research expert" status. Work in progress is my motto, which is why I am now moving from the receive mode to the broadcast mode where I share my experiences with accountants and financial advisors. I look forward to being a megaphone to broadcast what I view as an amazingly compelling story. I am confident that it will not be long before my status as a research expert will be replaced by that of a results expert. As I learned a long time ago, it's student first, teacher second, servant always.

Proverbs 11:24—One person gives freely, yet gains even more; another withholds unduly, but comes to poverty.

ON PURPOSE, WITH PASSION, BY DESIGN

Anyone who knows me understands that I am an extremely passionate person in every area of my life. I only write and speak about things that I understand and am truly passionate about. I wholeheartedly believe that the reason I have flourished in my profession is my commitment to serve with a purpose and with passion to genuinely make a difference in people's lives. My objective is to become my clients' most trusted advisor, with a foundation of ethics, trust, and competence. Admittedly, most advisors are more intelligent than I am, better marketers than I am, and more articulate than I am, but I will argue that I outserve every one of them, because I care so passionately about my clients.

Genuinely caring about one's clients is a crucial element of a prosperous business. People know when someone truly cares. You can't train someone to care. Either you care or you don't. Some folks think they can fake caring, as if they were using a tactic out of the book of prostitution. Sure, this may work for a while for some, but in the end their perverse ways will be discovered and they will fail.

I have always enjoyed the process much more than the proceeds of my profession, though I have learned to relish both. I am immeasurably more motivated by the advice I give than by any money I might earn. Making money is great, but living life is better. I work under the premise that to attract money is to not think about money. When we stop being self-centered and direct our heart and focus to the needs of others, good things will happen to us. When one believes enthusiastically in serving the needs of others without compromising principles and values for a few extra bucks, money normally follows.

I have been asked frequently, "How do I get your passion?" Unfortunately, I don't have the answer. What I do know is that passion is difficult, if not impossible, to manufacture. It won't just inexplicably emerge, and best of luck if you think you can fake it. It must emanate from the heart, and when we have acquired that natural enthusiastic passion, it fuels everything we do. I have become passionate about passion! The more I explore passion and its role in a meaningful and productive life, the more convinced I am that it's the key to unlocking powerful and sustained performance improvement, both at a personal and institutional level.

> When one believes enthusiastically in serving the needs of others without compromising principles and values for a few extra bucks, money normally follows.

For me, work is fun and I bring a great passion to it every day. I put my heart and soul into my job, and my clients and team appreciate it.

We have been told over and over that we have to find our purpose in life. I always had an issue with this. What does purpose look like? No one ever tells you. People simply tell you to find it, but how do you find something that seems to be so undefined? So let's first define passion and purpose, as well as success and the phrase "making a difference."

Here are my own definitions:

- Passion: intense emotion
- Purpose: the reason
- Success: continuing attainment of a worthy goal
- Making a difference: changing something negative into something positive

From my research, I have discovered that most folks and self-proclaimed gurus suggest that you need to find your purpose first before uncovering your passion. I argue that they are one and the same. Your life's passion is your life's purpose! If you don't know your purpose, find your passion. Passion will direct you to your purpose! Because passions are the lifelines to the heart, they connect with purpose in life. When you are connected to your passions, you feel happy, self-motivated, fulfilled, engaged, and worthwhile. And when you are disconnected from your true purpose, you become unhappy and irritable.

I believe with steadfast conviction that if you sincerely embrace your passion, success will follow. Since I use the word success quite a bit in this book, I want to bring your attention to the definition again. Notice that my definition says nothing about making a bunch of money or becoming a celebrity of sorts. Instead, success is the continuation of *your* worthy goal. Of course, if being rich and famous is your goal, then indeed, you can become successful in your own right, but I suggest that your "success" will be unfulfilling. I argue that money can never replace the passion to attain a worthy goal, as money does not bring happiness. Money, however, does provide the necessary resources to go narrow and deep with your passion until your heart is content.

So how do you find your passion? The moment you find something worth fighting for, you will find your purpose and passion. It then becomes easy to find the courage to fight all the inevitable battles to see your vision through. It was easy for me. My passion was born a long time ago when my heart got carried away with a purpose that took on a life of its own. My passion is to inspire, influence, and serve others who are driven to make a difference. I want to do well for myself in my career and finances while doing well for others. In my view, our goal should not be to be known for the services that we offer. Instead, let's be known for what we stand for. Folks are attracted to people who make a stand and are passionate about their views.

In my research for this book, I discovered time and again that many folks have trouble determining their passion. I submit that passion can't be found in the head because it lives in the heart. We must discover passion from the inside out. In other words, in time, the heart will tell the brain. When that time comes and you embrace your passion with gusto, you are on your way to success. In business, of course, there is always competition and your competitive advantage will come from having passion and purpose and a faithful desire to make a difference.

I staunchly believe that those who are passionate about their job, and enjoy the process more than the money, will succeed beyond their wildest dreams. Money follows passion! While many folks look forward to retiring and enjoying the golden years, I am enjoying the golden years while I am working! I am excited for Monday mornings as much as most people look forward to Friday afternoons. If you really love what you do, why would you want to retire? I genuinely don't feel that I work to make a living. I simply incorporate work into living. There is no finish line for me, no bell that ends the match. My life is a perpetual journey. Only when it's time for God to call me home will my pursuit be complete.

> I staunchly believe that those who are passionate about their job, and enjoy the process more than the money, will succeed beyond their wildest dreams. Money follows passion!

One reason I am motivated to go to work is that I manage my business and client relationships in an especially personal manner. Though I believe that I work harder than anyone I know, I have never felt that I have worked a day in my life. As I like to say, "I don't do this stuff for fun, but I have a lot of fun doing it!" I love being a financial advisor. I do it exceptionally well, and I am compensated remarkably well. I feel that I am getting paid to work on my hobby.

Proverbs 20:4—The sluggard does not plow in the autumn; he will seek at harvest and have nothing.

MAKING A DIFFERENCE

In Writing 101, we are taught to avoid clichés like the plague! I see it differently. Clichés are simple, easily recognizable phrases, and since I write to be understood, I will use them at my own peril. We have all heard it before: "Make a difference." Overused, sure, but it just happens to be one of my favorites. "Make a difference" declares that we are going to be the one to create a change, to be the difference. When we are a difference maker, we improve, refresh, transform, and encourage another person. I believe that the number-one attitude shared by the most influential people in the world is the burning desire to make a difference, as it is the energy that drives the passion to continually improve. Think about the last time that you made a difference, no matter how big or small, in someone's life. How did it make you feel? Did you have more gusto, vitality, and craving to do it again? Did it make you feel more alive? If you are like most people, giving warms the heart and satisfies the soul. When we devote ourselves to excellence in everything we do with the goal of truly making a difference in people's lives, we begin to feel a greater sense of purpose and enjoyment in life.

To emphasize this concept, a few years ago, MIT produced a study that measured the increase in brain function to different stimuli. What they discovered was that the third most effective stimulus was money and the second was sex. The stimulus that recorded the most brain activity was altruistic behavior! Doing noble, unselfish, philanthropic deeds created more excitement in the brain than money or sex. For me, there is no greater feeling in the world than to know I have made a difference in someone's life.

Working only for money is seldom a successful game plan. As Burchard proclaimed in his inspirational book *The Millionaire Messenger,* "if people spent as much time worrying about how to make a difference as they do about how they could make money, then they would soon find themselves rich beyond belief." I believe with utmost conviction that if we work under the premise of genuinely enjoying giving, offering constant unparalleled value, dedicating ourselves to excellence and activities that express honesty and trustworthiness, substantial rewards will present themselves somehow someday. It was Aristotle who said, "We are what we repeatedly do. Excellence, then, is not an act, but a habit."

If we truly try to make a difference in people's lives, while adhering to the law of reciprocity, positive and remarkable things usually emerge. I sense that companies and people who have a purpose and speak with emotion are motivated by the idea of making a difference. Of course, companies exist to make money, but while earning the greenback is undeniably of critical concern to most of us, I believe the primary reason for my existence is to make a difference. I have a fire-in-the-belly sense of purpose in my job that fueled me to compose this book. When you believe you are in business to make people's lives better, your job becomes enjoyable. I never lose focus on why I do what I do: to make a difference in people's lives. Sure, earning money is great but mattering is healthier.

In his classic book *Ultimate Success*, Frank Beaudine does a magnificent job of explaining the law of reciprocity. According to the author, "The law of reciprocity explains that when someone gives you something, you feel an obligation to give back." Although it is an obligation, people won't necessarily give back. Still, the more we give, the more we receive. I have lived by this attitude my entire professional life. I believe that to give and serve without expecting anything in return is the foundation of a successful and meaningful service model. This is how the law works; we can't expect anything in return when we give. Instead, we simply must have faith that, in the end, all will work out for the best.

Beaudine continues, "This is why the deliberate pursuit of reciprocity, in other words, approaching reciprocity as a transaction—I give value to you, therefore, you give equal or greater value back—does not work ... What does work is creating positive emotional experiences for others because you sincerely want to give them joy with no expectation for anything in return. This requires faith that, when you give with sincerity and for the right reasons, the universe has an amazing way of evening things out and paying you back many times over—sometimes directly, and sometimes indirectly." Unfortunately, far too many financial advisors ignore this universal truth when developing strategic professional alliances with centers of influence (CPAs). They provide a CPA with a referral or two and mistakenly expect one in return. They conduct themselves this way because they have no faith in the law of reciprocity. In essence, they are really "takers" disguised as "givers."

GIVERS GAIN!

Many Christians wonder what Jesus is saying in this short passage from the book of Matthew: "Ask and you shall receive." While the debate continues, I suggest that we consider something more straightforward: "Give and you shall receive." I argue that the giving attitude is a game changer. It's based on universal laws and principles that have stood the test of time. What is paramount to remember is that when we give, expecting a repayment, we will be disappointed. On the contrary, when we give with joy and give continuously, not expecting anything in return, we should benefit greatly.

Below is a wonderful and thought-provoking parable, *Two Seas in Palestine* by Bruce Barton (1886–1967), an American writer, advertising executive, and politician. The parable has become a classic in the literature of giving.

> There are two seas in Palestine. One is fresh, and fish are in it. Splashes of green adorn its banks. Trees spread their branches over it and stretch out their thirsty roots to sip of its healing waters. The River Jordan makes this sea with sparkling water from the

hills. So it laughs in the sunshine. And men build their houses near to it, and birds their nests; and every kind of life is happier because it is there.

The River Jordan flows on out into another sea. Here there is no splash of fish, no fluttering leaf, no song of birds, no children's laughter. Travelers choose another route, unless on urgent business. The air hangs heavy above its water, and neither man nor beast nor fowl will drink. What makes this mighty difference in these neighbor seas? Not the River Jordan. It empties the same good water into both. Not the soil in which they lie; not in the country round about.

This is the difference.

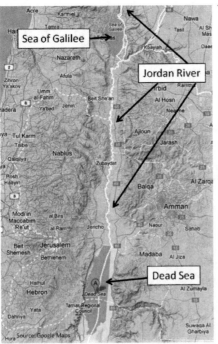

The Sea of Galilee receives but does not keep the Jordan. For every drop that flows into it, another drop flows out. The giving and receiving go on in equal measure. The other sea is shrewder, hoarding its income jealously. It will not be tempted into any generous impulse. Every drop it gets, it keeps. The Sea of Galilee gives and lives. This other sea gives nothing. It is named Dead. There are two kinds of people in this world. There are two seas in Palestine.

Which sea are you? A sea that gives and lives, or a sea that gives nothing and only keeps? Most people often begin their journey as "Dead Sea people." At least I know I did. I was a "miserly banker." As I strive to be a "Sea of Galilee person," I have become "a recovering banker." Even from the geography of the Holy Land of Israel, we learn deep lessons on how to conduct our lives. Perhaps we make a living by what we receive, but we make a life by what we give. As American President Calvin Coolidge said, "No person was ever honored for what he received. Honor has been the reward for what he gave."

CHAPTER 4

The Ten-Step Commitment Ladder

The COMMITMENT Ladder

M any people talk about wanting to achieve something. They are desperately seeking advice, success strategies, and how-to material. They have lofty goals, dreams, and aspirations, but what far too many people don't have is the commitment to see it through. These people perhaps get fired up when reading or hearing something motivational and/or inspirational. They are ready to conquer the world, but over and over again, this excitement ends in disappointment and they are back to the status quo.

Why is it that this scenario plays itself repeatedly? I argue that these well-intended folks simply never climb to the top of the commitment ladder. The higher we climb on the ladder, the more our purpose and passion take on a life of their own, which results in delivering more value to our clients. When our clients receive more value, they become loyal, not just satisfied, clients. Then they give us more business, and then the money flows. When the money flows, we become more passionate, which creates more value, which results in more money. Guess what happens next? That's right, we get even more passionate, and you know the rest of the story. Truthfully, climbing to the top of the commitment ladder is dreamlike.

Moreover, I propose that the service we provide, coupled with the sacrifice of doing what others will not do, is the key to the journey of success. H. L. Hunt, a man who rose from a bankrupt cotton farmer in the 1930s to a multibillionaire when he died, was asked during a TV interview what advice he could give to others who wanted to be financially successful. He said only two things are required. First, you must decide exactly what it is you want to accomplish. Most people never do that in their entire lives. And second, you must determine what price you will pay to get it and resolve to pay that price. I believe Mr. Hunt is saying that when you are clear about what you want, your subconscious and conscious minds work in harmony toward the same mission. Let's not forget that it all begins with clarity on your current situation and clarity on your future situation. When this is determined, you simply close the gap by committing yourself to getting it done!

Having the burning desire to accomplish something is more important than all the talent in the world.

When I am asked to speak, my preferred topic is the "Commitment Ladder to Business Success." All too often, success seekers look for the elevator, not realizing that you must take the stairs to success. Unfortunately, most people don't have the dedication and perseverance to see a meaningful venture through to the end. They toss in the towel and justify their lack of tenacity while they continue their march toward mediocrity. At the end of the day, you are the one who gets to choose how you want show up in life. If you want to man up and meet the challenges head on, it won't be stress-free, but it will be worth the effort every time!

"There is one weakness in people for which there is no remedy. It is the universal weakness of lack of ambition," Napoleon Hill wrote. If you truly want to position your firm for the future while creating additional success, both personally and financially, this chapter may perhaps be the most essential. One of the primary reasons this is a hot subject for me is that I am a chronic and recovering overachiever. I am not naturally gifted. I never had the raw talent to compete, but I would always be willing to outhustle my competition. Paying the price for success was never a problem for me. In fact, I welcomed it. Although I have many shortcomings, I never felt pressure while building my business, because I knew what I was trying to accomplish and had the commitment to see it through. I adapted. I improvised. I overcame. As Peyton Manning says, "Pressure is something you feel when you don't know what the hell you are doing."

While reading an article authored by Nancy Fox, founder of Business Fox, a coaching and training program, I stumbled upon the essence of what it means to be a hustler. "If you are interested in success, you will do what is convenient. If you are committed to success, you will do whatever the hell is necessary."

CLIMB THE LADDER: HOW HIGH CAN WE GO?

Step 1: Desire. Either we have an all-consuming, pulsating burning aspiration, or we don't. It's not something we can borrow, buy, or find at a seminar or in a book. We can only find it in ourselves. If it's there, we will know it, because it will motivate us until we reach our goals, and at the same time, it will drive us crazy in the process.

We will tolerate the stress, the hardships, and the shortcomings so that one day we can experience the incomparable high that accompanies achievement. The proper combination of internal motivation and proven systems is just about a guaranteed winner. I say this with great belief: Having the burning desire to accomplish something is more important than all the talent in the world. Burning desire is what launches all accomplishments.

Step 2: Character and integrity. The way I see it, character and integrity trumps credentials every time. I believe character and

" I know the difference between right and wrong, but it hasn't held me back. "

integrity are two of the most important qualities one can possess. I define character as simply doing what is right, because it is right. In my practice, doing what is right because it is right is non-negotiable. I consider it an investment in my reputation and peace of mind. Confucius said, "To know what is right and not to do it is the worst cowardice." A good measure of character and integrity is giving up something of personal value in order to do what is just. Small actions are often excellent clues to true character. For me, how we treat others who can't help us is a great clue to our character.

Dave Anderson's *Learn to Lead* blog offers a more academic view of the difference between integrity and character. Allow me to paraphrase a portion of Anderson's blog, dated September 6, 2010:

> Character and integrity are both important, but they are not synonymous. In fact, integrity without the right character can spell trouble. This is why it's important to first determine someone's character before we ask that person to live with integrity. Here is the dictionary's description of character: "the combination of qualities or features that distinguishes one person, group, or thing from another. A distinguishing feature or attribute, as of an individual, group, or category." Character can be thought of as someone's moral and ethical code. It is a combination of inside traits that determine outward behavior. Now look at the definition of integrity: "steadfast adherence to a strict moral or ethical code." When people have character and integrity, they have a moral and ethical code and their integrity drives them to live according to that code. Thus, those who live with integrity, live according to their moral values.

People who possess these virtues understand that their own character and integrity will always be remembered far longer than the amount of business they generate. If we are known for what we stand for rather than the product we offer, we attract folks with similar principals and beliefs who want to be part of our team. Let's not heed the words of wisdom from Groucho Marx, who said, "These are my principles, and if you don't like them ... well, I have others."

Proverbs 24:10—If you faint in the day of adversity,
your strength is small.

Step 3: Persistence. I remind myself frequently that I have not failed until I quit. In *Think and Grow Rich*, Hill includes this thought, "Every successful person finds that great success lies just beyond the point when they are convinced their idea is not going to work." This is when you can really see who has what it takes to be big. And where the men are separated from the boys. Success waits for those of us who can hang on just a little bit longer and endure the pain just a bit more, those who simply do not give up.

Persistence compensates for lack of talent, lack of intelligence, even lack of salesmanship, as victory usually goes to the one who is most resilient. After being knocked down, we must be able to get up time and time again. We must be persistent even when we are physically and mentally exhausted. Vince Lombardi, the Green Bay Packer's legendary coach, once said, "fatigue makes cowards of us all." When we think about giving up because things are becoming too demanding, or we find that we just have trouble moving the ball forward, fatigue is setting in. We can't allow it to make cowards of us. It is easy to give up. That is what most people do. These people may be brilliant, creative, and capable, but they fail to reach their goal because of their absence of "stick-to-it-iveness." "One should acquire the tenacity of a bulldog, and refuse to be shaken off a thing once he has fixed its attention and desire upon it," Napoleon Hill wrote. In the end, the story about gazelles in South Africa encapsulates my view about never giving up. Every morning in South Africa, a gazelle wakes up knowing it must run faster than the fastest lion or be killed. Every morning, a lion wakes up knowing it must outrun the slowest gazelle or starve to death. It doesn't matter if we are gazelles or lions. When the sun comes up, we had better be running.

Step 4: Adversity. One of the most common causes of failure is quitting when overtaken by temporary defeat. When difficulties strike, the easiest and most logical thing to do is to quit, but not if you are former Marine lieutenant and motivational speaker Clede McClary, who says that you must FIDO (forget it, drive on!). In other words, fuhgeddaboudit! Successful people FIDO, because they embrace failure and don't allow roadblocks to stop them from accomplishing their dreams. They understand that failure is important! They view hardships as life lessons, an attitude, not an outcome. If you show me a successful person, I'll show you someone who has suffered mountains of setbacks and encountered countless roadblocks on the climb to the top. Such people are successful because they overcame obstacles and learned from them. They prepare and anticipate setbacks because they know the messenger of misery will be arriving soon. When misfortunes present themselves, the pros go through them, around them, above them, or below them. They know that adversity is part of life's learning process. It is the catalyst for learning.

> When misfortunes present themselves, the pros go through it, around it, above it or below it. They know that adversity is part of life's learning process.

When hardships emerge, I habitually struggle with frustration, anger, and disappointment. I get down on myself, but I don't stay down. Staying down is for losers. Instead, I heed the words of wisdom from author and minister Dr. Norman Vincent Peale, who said; "If you have no problems at all, I warn you, you are in grave jeopardy.

You are on your way out and you don't know it. Perhaps what you had better do is immediately go to your room and shut the door and get down on your knees and pray to the Lord, 'Lord, please; look don't you trust me anymore? Give me some problems!'" We all get our share of setbacks, so let's not try to duck them. Success is tough, folks. We have to strap in and meet misfortune head on. In other words, when adversity comes, it is no time for timidity. I recently read that the Chinese ideogram for the word crisis is composed of two characters. One represents danger; the other signifies opportunity.

Proverbs 24:10—If you faint in the day of adversity, your strength is small.

Step 5: Learning. Will we continually sharpen the saw? According to author and businessman Steven Covey, sharpen the saw means "preserving and enhancing the greatest asset you have: you. It means having a balanced program for self-renewal in the four areas of your life: physical, social/emotional, mental, and spiritual." How we feed our mind is every bit as critical to how we feed our bodies. All the successful people I know or have known are devoted readers. They apply the "CANI" philosophy to become better. They simply need to know. They are inherently inquisitive.

According to personal development guru Jim Rohn, "Formal education will earn you a living. Self-education will earn you a fortune." To put it another way: it is more important to work harder on ourselves than on our occupation. I read somewhere that Rohn recommends making time to read just one hour per day. If you do this rather minor activity, you will finish a good-size book in about a week. In ten years you would have read 520 books and in 20 years more than 1,000! Imagine the knowledge you would have after reading 1,000 books. Imagine the enthusiasm and conviction you would possess on the various subjects. The amazing thing is all it takes is one hour a day. I love what renowned author and speaker Jeffrey Gitomer has to say regarding learning: "College education prepares you to play Jeopardy and Trivial Pursuit. The rest of what you need to learn about your success, you have to learn on your own." Finally, a quote from the legendary UCLA basketball coach John Wooden: "If I am through learning, I am through." I am often asked, "How do you have the time to read, given all that you do?" The answer is quite simple; it is never a time issue for me. It's a priority issue. I simply make reading a priority. The bottom line is that there is never enough time for everything, but there is always enough time for the important things.

Proverbs 24:4—By knowledge the rooms are filled with all precious and pleasant riches.

Step 6: Mentoring. Throughout human history and well before there were books and institutions of higher learning, people would humbly seek out the master and learn from him. In other words, they sit on the shoulders of giants and model their success. Find someone who is doing or has accomplished what you want to achieve and model that person. It would be foolish not to take advantage of this priceless opportunity that could provide you with an incredible blueprint for your success.

A Chinese proverb states, "Mentors know the road ahead. Ask those coming back." I urge you not to be a Lone Ranger and try to figure things out on your own. Learn from those who have already walked the path before you. Successful people leave clues and it is our job to uncover them. There is an old saying: "Watch the man ahead of you and you will soon learn why he is ahead." I learned a long time ago that it is far more productive to imitate a successful person than to envy him. Even Yogi Berra had an interesting take on mentorship. Berra said baseball celebrity Bill Dickey was "learning me all his experience."

Proverbs 27:17—Iron sharpens iron,
and one man sharpens another.

Step 7: The little things. I offer that obsessing over the little things is what separates the achievers from the sustainers, the great from the good. I believe without hesitation that it is the little things in life that we perform consistently, day in and day out, that will generate the breakthroughs to which we aspire. We all fall prey to ignoring the little things that we know are important but that, at the time, seem somewhat insignificant. To illustrate this, reading ten pages of a self-development book every day doesn't sound like such a big deal. However, that's 70 pages a week or 280 pages a month, which works out to an average of about 12 books a year—just by reading ten pages a day. It is akin to attending a few semesters of school per year. The more attention we give to perceived irrelevant things, the more likely we will recognize how relevant they really are. Little things not only make a difference, they make all the difference. Even the largest door will yield to a small shove, all because of a couple of little hinges. My personal experience has proved that it is never just one thing that creates victory. Instead, it is the willingness to continue performing the small but important things repeatedly and forever. I call obsessing over the little things "winning by inches."

Step 8: The extra mile. The great companies overdeliver. In business and life, most people trek down the road most traveled. I describe this as the first mile, the complacency mile, which is rather smooth and uneventful. Relatively few people will travel down the potholed second mile, the extra mile. This is the road that is not well traveled. The first mile is a relatively easy drive and most people handle it with few problems. It is the second mile, that extra mile, where you take your company from the sea of sameness to a firm that is truly different from all others. Most people won't take the extra mile because it is a difficult and challenging voyage. What is interesting is that folks who take the extra mile are so driven by their internal belief system that they don't consider the extra mile as being anything but normal. At its core, it is just two miles.

Even so, when you go down the extra mile, you go beyond just being good. You give more, care more, work more, sharpen the saw more, and do more for your clients, friends, and family. You are doing things that others won't do. By providing consistent evidence that you always give and do more than required, over time, that journey of the extra mile builds a rock-solid foundation of trust with your clients, friends, and family. Napoleon Hill said it best, "When you truly believe that the habit of going the extra mile is the only acceptable way to conduct yourself in your dealings with others, when you are driven by a burning desire to serve your fellow man, you will be rewarded both financially and professionally."

Step 9: Investing. Will we invest money in our business? I am a huge fan of Michael E. Gerber and his E-Myth books. The E-Myth is short for the entrepreneurial myth, which Gerber explains this way: "Most businesses fail to fulfill their potential because most people starting their own business are not entrepreneurs at all. They actually are what I call technicians suffering from entrepreneurial seizure. In short, the E-Myth says that most financial advisors and CPAs don't own a true business, most own a job." The highly successful author and business consultant continues, "The E-Myth philosophy says that the key to transforming your practice into a successful enterprise is knowing how to transform yourself from a successful accounting technician into a successful entrepreneur." How do you like this one? Many industry gurus refer to an entrepreneurial accountant as an oxymoron! Concerning Gerber's point, a highly regarded consultant told me that if I want to see a small increase in my business, I should change my behavior. If I want to witness a quantum leap in my business, I should change my attitude!

If you think about it, people normally do not invest money in a job. They simply put in the required hours at work and go home. Entrepreneurs, on the other hand, see their occupation as one big idea that they continually improve. This desire to constantly advance usually involves financial investment in their business. The subject of business "investment" often has me shaking my head in bewilderment. I repeatedly have witnessed financial advisor and accountants spending thousands of dollars on arguably frivolous things such as boats, cars, wines, clothes, and so on. Yet they balk at the price of a new computer, software, employing the services of a consultant, or giving their staff a raise. If we want to be successful and take our business to the next level, we must do what successful people do: invest money in our big idea!

Step 10: Risk. You are allowed to fail but are not allowed to not try! In football, they call it the end around play. In warfare, it's known as a flanking maneuver. The world chess masters watch for the wing attack. No matter what it is called, it's about taking risk. Every prosperous person I know has taken calculated gambles and made sacrifices. It seems to be a common denominator among thriving companies and people. They are on the cutting edge. They are trendsetters, not followers. Many folks are afraid to take chances because they expect the ridicule that often accompanies risk taking.

I believe that sarcasm, laughter, ridicule, and mockery come from discouraged human beings who play it safe and won't risk anything in order to reach their aspirations. I simply refer to them as losers. They spend most of their time criticizing and nitpicking others. They don't want to see others do well while they continue to stagnate because of their status-quo-hugging thinking. These people should be avoided like an airport toilet! As Oscar Wilde said, "Ridicule is the tribute paid to the genius by the mediocrities." Winners are much different; they walk quietly, but carry a big stick. They differentiate themselves from the crowd by feeling the fear but moving forward nonetheless. These folks know they can't steal second base by keeping a foot on first.

I am closing this chapter with a powerful poem, "Will to Win," written by American poet, Berton Braley (1882–1966). It has become a signature close of one of my favorite motivational speakers, Les Brown. It epitomizes the commitment mentality. Brown's paraphrase of Braley's poem:

> If you want a thing bad enough to go out and fight for it, to work day and night for it, to give up your time, your peace and your sleep for it. If all that you dream and scheme is about it, and life seems useless and worthless without it and you would gladly sweat for it and fret for it and plan for it and lose all your terror of the opposition for it. And if you simply go after the thing that you want with all of your capacity, strength, and sagacity, faith, hope and confidence and stern pertinacity if neither cold, poverty, famine

or sickness in pain or body can keep you away from the thing that you want. If dogged and grim you besiege and beset, with the help of God you will get it.

CHAPTER 5

We've Just Lost Cabin Pressure!

When an airplane loses cabin pressure, it is a serious and life-threatening predicament. For example, at 30,000 feet there is not enough oxygen to keep us going. We will lose consciousness in about 30 seconds as cerebral hypoxia sets in, and then we are on our free flight to heaven. Well, this is how I felt when I got the word that CPAs could begin to accept commissions. I couldn't catch my breath. I couldn't get enough oxygen. I couldn't imagine competing with the client's most trusted advisor!

" Here's where accounting went all ethical on us. "

In 1985, the role of a CPA was well defined and limited in its capacity for financial advice. For accountants to provide assistance over and beyond the imposed limitations was considered inconceivable and highly unethical. As most agree, the industry has evolved beyond recognition from the time when the 1990 Federal Trade Commission order required the American Institute of Certified Public Accountants (AICPA) to lift its ban on the acceptance of commissions by CPAs.

"Oh no, say it ain't so" were the words I uttered when I first learned of the devastating news (for financial advisors). I thought my days were numbered as a financial advisor. Not only are CPAs quite possibly my clients' most important decision makers, but they now also could do what I did. Although I realized not every accountant was cut out to be a financial advisor, I nonetheless considered myself to be in a heap of trouble.

We all know who has the most influence on businesses and individuals: you, the CPA. I assumed that if the so-called back-office bean counters truly embraced this opportunity to become their client's wealth manager, the sky would be the limit for their practices. But wait a minute. What about the ethics of CPAs accepting commissions? Do CPAs really want to play in the same game with financial advisors? Any wise person will tell you the importance of the company you keep.

THE ETHICS OF REVENUE SHARING: AN OXYMORON?

The idea that the accountants might peddle financial products for commission seemed like turning left and right at the same time. It was thought that it just couldn't happen. Heck, it wasn't long ago the accounting profession could not advertise! Such a scenario would have been unthinkable and illegal before 1990. Nevertheless, when CPAs were allowed to accept commissions and fees, everyone expected our friends from Wall Street to unearth tactics to get in on the action. That is exactly what happened in 1998 when Salomon Smith Barney and Merrill Lynch established programs to compensate CPAs who referred clients to their asset management businesses.

While these revenue-sharing arrangements have been around for 16 years, quite a few CPAs continue to cringe at the thought of a CPA accepting a referral fee. Perhaps it's because they are led by a code of ethics that maintains that competent and ethical professionals should refer clients to each other for no compensation, simply because it is the right thing to do. As I am sure you know, the subject of CPAs accepting commissions and/or fees has been a hotly contested issue for the past 24 years. Yet, each year an increasing number of accountants discover avenues to generate more money through commissions and fees.

Many advocates of the revenue-sharing arrangement view this scenario as merely a means of outsourcing. Their claim is that financial advisors outsource many aspects of their business. Why shouldn't CPAs have the same opportunity? "Many CPA firms do not have the internal resources to offer financial planning, investment management or asset custody to their clients," says Bedda D'Angelo, whose advisory firm, Fiscal Conditioning Inc., dba Fiduciary Services, is based in Chapel Hill, North Carolina. "A referral arrangement is another way to outsource services that the firm is unable to provide internally. Most CPAs who engage in the practice carefully profile and screen the planner they refer their clients to. It deeply concerns me when members of one profession make subjective value judgments on what constitutes ethical conduct in the practice of another profession."

HERE THEY COME AGAIN

During the past couple of decades, the media has regularly suggested that CPAs would be the next most influential group of financial advisors. Virtually everyone accepts that there is an enormous opportunity for CPAs to capitalize on the current trend that is still disputably in its infancy, but this move has not been without its challenges and skeptics. The risks and responsibilities involved in creating and overseeing a wealth-management practice regularly yanked resources away from CPAs' core businesses, and even caused significant disagreements between partners. Many CPAs were either tempted by vendors and/or broker dealers who did not understand the CPA mindset, or they allowed greed to cloud their better judgment.

Although there are many CPAs/financial advisors who have enjoyed incredible success over the years, things never accelerated in the way that so many predicted. The results continue to be a huge disappointment compared with the perceived potential. At the outset, many accounting professionals contended with numerous unexpected roadblocks. In response, some abandoned their effort and others simply pursued financial services on a limited, opportunistic basis.

Regardless of the path that was taken, many CPAs found themselves in a nightmare situation as they quickly learned that establishing a wealth-management practice was much more intricate than simply hanging an "open for business" sign on their front door. In the final analysis, the transition from tax preparer to wealth manager can reasonably be characterized as a lot of fuss about nothing and all the hype was nothing but a big tease—at least until now.

If the industry authorities are correct, it may be a good time to sing the lyrics of Bob Dylan's 1964 hit song, "The Times They Are A-Changin'." According to *Accounting Today* editor-in-chief Daniel Hood, "There was a great deal of interest a decade ago in CPA firms taking up financial planning ... but it turns out that not that many firms really went all the way in creating a formal planning and wealth-management practice. As firms started exploring this option again, they have a lot of room to expand, and can learn a lot from the firms that have pioneered these services, which is what we're trying to uncover with our surveys."

My research revealed that accounting firms that had been just dabbling in financial services are coming back to the starting line to pursue the initiative with greater commitment, enthusiasm, and financial resources in order to be more competitive. Many self-proclaimed gurus are suggesting that we are entering the second big boom in financial services offered by accounting professionals.

You have a unique advantage and should capitalized on it, as your competency, integrity, and objectivity regarding tax issues will differentiate you from other CPAs which ultimately will allow you to control most of the business and remain your client's most trusted advisor. On the surface, financial planning and wealth management seems to be a profession similar to accounting, but I suggest they are much more different than alike.

> Most people admire and willingly follow those who are trustworthy, honest, ethical, and who live by principles.

Planning and wealth management require heavy-duty relationship building and analytical skills. The delivery of personal wealth advisory services involves legal and regulatory issues different from, and often more complex than, those of audit, accounting, or tax services, not to mention the steep and long learning curve. Many CPAs envisioned a new source of revenue and potentially more-meaningful relationships with clients but were blindsided and surprised by the complexities of managing clients' assets. Additionally, the overhead related to operating a wealth-management business can be overwhelming. It is common to find CPAs exiting the financial advisory business not long after initiating such a service. Mistakes in the highly competitive, volatile, and regulated industry can, and often do, lead to unhappy clients who eventually fire their CPA.

The following survey results underscore my concern for CPAs who attempt to develop wealth-management integration on their own. Here is what CPAs have said were the primary reasons for terminating their in-house wealth-management services:

1. Eighty-six percent said they never fully committed to the business.
2. Seventy-one percent said they did not have the experience or expertise to be an advisor.
3. Sixty-seven percent said they were never able to move beyond the low-hanging fruit.

Although the above results are not encouraging for those going the Lone Ranger route, the rewards of offering wealth advisory services can be substantial and immediate. Unless you are prepared to acquire the education, talents, and experience necessary to serve your tax client in the wealth-management arena, you are positioning yourself for disappointment. The task of wealth-management integration is a daunting assignment to undertake on your own. I hear numerous stories of CPAs recommending specific investments to their clients, only to see the market tank and witness their clients' portfolio values plummet. Of course, the inevitable calls arrive from the disgruntled clients, and the CPA now has to explain and hand hold. It doesn't take many of these situations before the CPAs wave the white flag and surrender.

Of course, there are those CPAs who have embraced wealth management and all its nuances and are seeing magnificent success. While it might read as though I have little conviction that CPAs can flourish in the financial services industry, the opposite is actually true. There are many natural-born rainmakers among the CPA crowd. I know some of them and have listened to many sharing their secrets of success, but they are in the minority.

My position is straightforward and blunt: Follow the advice of the legendary Warren Buffett and "stick to what you know." Focus on what you do best and leverage the rest. If you want to be successful as a CPA, stop performing work as a financial advisor. If being a financial advisor is your desire, quit performing tax work. Trying to be both a top-shelf tax expert and sought-after financial advisor will ultimately be detrimental to most practices and clients.

"The only way to get out of the 'rat race' is to prove your proficiency at both accounting and investing, arguably two of the most difficult subjects to master," wrote Robert Kiyosaki, author of *Rich Dad Poor Dad*. As the quote suggests, this stuff is difficult and time consuming. Let's remain focused on our strengths. Trying to stay on top of all the pertinent and required information to become the best at both jobs is overwhelming, to say the least.

I reason that it is in clients' best interests to receive investment advice from their trustworthy financial advisor and accounting advice from their most trusted advisor, you! If you focus on providing tax services well and engage specialists in other areas of financial planning, the quality of your work will improve and you will differentiate yourself from the crowded marketplace. Strategic alliance and collaboration are the buzzwords that will prepare the CPA firms of the future. The partnership of a CPA and a wealth manager is the future of both of our industries.

COMPREHENSIVE, FEE-BASED, WEALTH-MANAGEMENT PROCESS

Although many CPAs have only loosely embraced a wealth-management service for their clients, there are those who have gone narrow and deep with the service and have been remarkably successful. These CPAs recognize that providing a financial service deepens their client relationships much more than tax return preparation does. You become the resource your clients go to for all their financial needs, from retirement and estate planning to investment and risk management planning. Regardless of the channel that you select when incorporating financial services into your practice, the comprehensive, holistic, fee-based approach has proven to be the most successful.

What do affluent investors want most from their financial advisors? The answer is simply to have complete trust in them. I don't have to tell you that we are in a crisis of trust and trust is our most precious possession. Stephen M. R. Covey, author of *The Speed of Trust: The One Thing that Changes Everything*, says, "When trust goes down, speed will also go down and cost will go up. When trust goes up, speed will also go up and cost will go down." An atmosphere of trust creates greater efficiency and effectiveness. Trust is everything! It's not a technique. It's not a sales tactic. It must be earned and when it happens, the money will follow. Instead of viewing this crisis of trust matter as a negative, let's see it as a huge opportunity.

Here is a simple but noteworthy story regarding the impact of trust and how one business owner separated himself from his competition. Author David Horsager tells the story in his brilliant book titled *The Trust Edge: How Top Leaders Gain Faster Results, Deeper Relationships, and a Stronger Bottom Line.* It is about a street vendor named Ralph who sells donuts and coffee on the streets of Manhattan. What is unique about Ralph's business model is that he allows his customers to make their own change. On a typical morning, a regular customer will order a coffee and donut from Ralph for $1.75. The customer drops $2 in the bin and takes his 25 cents and moves on to allow the next customer to do the same. Ralph doesn't touch the money. He is too busy pouring coffee and fetching donuts to worry about money.

I am sure some people take advantage of Ralph's trustworthiness, but I suspect he makes up for it in efficiency. As the story is told, Ralph does about twice the business of his competitor with the same resources, and his customers get their coffee and donuts in half the time they would from a competitor. You can be sure that his customers love Ralph and the way he does business. When an environment of trust is created, good things start to happen. Ralph has an incredible reputation and business, all because he delivers trust and fairness.

The top financial advisors earn millions of dollars and have incredibly loyal clients. They did not reach the pinnacle of their profession because they are the best salesperson or possess the greatest closing techniques. The fact is that their clients see them as trusted advisors who have their best interest at heart. These highly successful advisors, for the most part, employ a disciplined, organized, fee-based approach to asset management. I believe that an effective and prudent investment strategy does not have to be difficult. Investing is rather simple, but it isn't easy. I have discovered that when clients don't understand something, it is hard to trust the information or the person delivering it.

I credit my six tenets of a proven investment strategy for my success in managing clients' money:

Gold Standard of Wealth-Management Process

1. Own quality investments (no speculation).
2. Diversify your investments (asset allocation).
3. Invest for the long term (minimum three to five years).
4. Hire professionals to manage your assets (don't do it yourself).
5. Implement a transparent, cost-effective investment strategy (fees matter).
6. Don't allow the "tax tail to wag the dog" (make decisions based on the merits of the investment strategy first and then look at the taxes).

Gold Standard for Engaging the Client

It is also imperative that you demonstrate evidence of careful, reasoned, and thoughtful planning and implementation. For instance:

Step 1: Current situation evaluation (CSE): interview to determine if you and your client are a good fit.

Step 2: Data gathering: collect pertinent personal and financial information from client.

Step 3: Analyze: put the puzzle together by reviewing client's current positions and asset allocation.

Step 4: Solution: provide a comprehensive investment strategy to accomplish client's goals and objectives.

Step 5: Implement: put the plan into action.

Step 6: Monitor and serve: establish ongoing periodic reviews to determine if adjustments should be employed. Additionally, provide exceptional service in which you go over and beyond the call of duty.

In the thought-provoking book *The Ensemble Practice: A Team-Based Approach to Building a Superior Wealth Management Firm*, author Philip Palaveev makes an interesting comparison with the fee-based approach to portfolio management: "As clients started to pay to have a percentage of their assets managed for the ongoing advice of the professional, suddenly there was a need for a completely new type of organization, new type of skills, and ultimately a new type of culture and values." He compares it to the advent of agriculture, when "growing became more important than hunting and cultivating more productive than gathering. Nurturing and preserving existing client relationships produces a reliable and predictable stream of revenues for advisors and favors those that can retain clients rather than jumping from one client and transaction to the next ... The more recurring and predictable the revenues are, the more the practice can have the patience to cultivate relationships and to train and develop staff. The more the practice has to constantly search for new revenues, the less likely it is to have the long-term focus to build and develop relationships."

I believe that this type of agreement is not only good business, but it's also the professional and ethical way to conduct business.

STRIVING TO BE JUST LIKE YOU

Whom do we trust more, firefighters or stock brokers? How about librarians or attorneys? Nurses or sales people? The extent of our trust depends greatly on whether we perceive a potential conflict of interest, which can create skepticism or lack of trust. This underscores why we trust our firefighters, librarians, and nurses more than we trust people who are selling something.

Since becoming a financial advisor in 1985, I was determined to be among the firefighters of my profession. Although I succeeded to a large extent, I quickly learned that the most-trusted-advisor designation was unquestionably owned by the client's CPA. Here I am, 28 years later, and essentially nothing has changed. Even after big accounting scandals such as those of Enron and Arthur Andersen, CPAs continue to enjoy the highly coveted distinction of being the most trusted advisor, according to public opinion polls. I marvel at the trust that is displayed between a client and his CPA, and how the vast majority of clients view their accountants. In observing the accounting profession, I saw proof that earning the client's trust was paramount and that trust is the foundation on which client relationships thrive.

In a 2011 Gallup poll, accountants placed highest among members of the general public who were asked which business professionals they most trusted. Accountants earned an average approval rating of 49 percent, placing them first among business professionals, and ahead of bankers by 25 percent, lawyers by 19 percent, and stockbrokers by 12 percent. Since 1976, when the poll was started, accountants have consistently ranked first among the business professionals viewed as the most trusted by the public. In these same polls, I frequently find that the financial service industry brings up the rear.

CPAs' earned reputation of independence, integrity, and objectivity, along with their strict adherence to a code of conduct, has enabled them to become clients' most trusted advisor. I consider this to be among the highest honors one can obtain. You are the authority and perhaps the go-to people. That is priceless! But it comes with an enormous responsibility, as I consider it the accountant's duty to use this privileged status to provide the client with the very best advice and service possible.

Proverbs 28:20—A trustworthy person will receive many blessings, but one rushing to get rich will not go unpunished.

The trade journal *Investment News* made a very interesting comparison between our two industries in a February 5, 2012, column: "Financial advisors can learn a valuable lesson from accountants about professionalism and adherence to a fiduciary standard. As most of the financial service community debates whether to extend fiduciary standards to cover everyone who provides advice, CPAs already operate their practices two steps beyond that debate. More importantly, many financial services representatives are not guided by any professional code at all, but rather focus more narrowly on regulatory compliance." That's a tough act to follow. Nevertheless, I have been on a laser-focused, 28-year mission to be just like you, my clients' most trusted advisor. It is a thread woven through everything that I do.

Although I place CPAs on the proverbial pedestal when it comes to trust, it troubles me greatly that CPAs are viewed by their clients as impartial and with no hidden agenda, while advice given by financial advisors is frequently deemed questionable and tainted by the potential commission that is generated. Furthermore, I argue that, just as in our profession, there exists a conflict of interest. Isn't hourly billing a direct conflict of interest? Clients pay for a service they want performed correctly and quickly, while their CPA may prefer to slow it down a bit in order to clock up time. Is this not a potential conflict? Doesn't hourly billing punish CPAs for introducing, for example, technology advancements that allow them to perform tasks faster and more efficiently? Are CPAs not rewarded for being inefficient? As a general rule, the longer CPAs take to complete a task, the more money they make. The bottom line is that charging by the hour does not focus on value; it focuses on time. How is that in the client's best interest? Paul Dunn and Ronald J. Baker, authors of the riveting book *The Firm of the Future: A Guide for Accountants, Lawyers, and Other Professional Services* (published by Wiley), boldly state, "The firm of the future does not have hourly rates; it has prices, set in advance of work being done." Now that eliminates the conflict of interest!

There are unethical CPAs as there are unethical financial advisors. Yet the public's perception is that a CPA can be trusted much more than a financial advisor can be. From my viewpoint, however, financial advisors are the reason that CPAs are trusted so much. Financial advisors simply lost the public's trust a long time ago because of one word: greed. We have nobody to blame but ourselves, and it has been and will continue to be a long uphill battle to win back the public's trust, but we must do so, as the road to success is directly predicated on the trust we develop with our clients along the way.

I have been pursuing trust since the day I became a financial advisor. My goal was and still is simple and straightforward: I wanted to earn my client's trust, grow my client's trust, and keep my client's trust. In the end, I want to be my client's most trusted adviser. Most people admire and willingly follow those who are trustworthy, honest, and ethical and who live by principles. This is the enviable position that CPAs possess. I applaud the accounting profession for having such an impressive reputation, and I have a glimmer of hope that, one day, the financial services industry will enjoy a similar status. In the meantime, we must continue to operate ethically, develop trust, and make a positive difference in our clients' lives, one step at a time.

> Trust is everything! It's not a technique. It's not a sales tactic. It must be earned and when it happens, the money will follow

CHAPTER 6

Houston, We Have a Problem

Another of my favorite clichés is "Houston, we have a problem." During the Apollo 13 moon flight on April 13, 1970, an oxygen tank ruptured and the landing had to be aborted. A quarter-century later, in the movie *Apollo 13*, astronaut Jack Swigert's words—which actually were "Houston, we've had a problem here"—were altered to the present tense in the script.

Now back to the purpose of this book. I do not want to appear overly dramatic, but, for CPAs who are used to and content with the status quo, I proclaim there is a ticking time bomb in their practices. After several years of warnings, the explosive is not far from detonation. Without question, the tax preparation business is becoming more of a commodity every year. If you don't believe me, check out IRS.gov. The number of self-prepared e-filed tax returns increased 55 percent from 2009 to 2013. In 2009, e-file returns accounted for 23 percent of tax returns, while in 2013 they accounted for 34 percent. In 2013, an incredible 43.5 million people prepared their own taxes electronically. I suggest, "Houston, we have a problem"!

Fifty-four years ago, the *Harvard Business Review* published an important article by Theodore Levitt, a lecturer in business administration at Harvard Business School. The article, "Marketing Myopia," became one of the most influential business articles of its time. Another word for myopia is *near-sightedness*. In the business world, myopia is a short-sighted business strategy that could lead to business failure. "Marketing Myopia" suggests that businesses will do better in the end if they concentrate on meeting client's needs rather than on providing their customary services. In the article, Levitt introduced the famous question that I believe all CPAs and financial advisors need to ask themselves, "What business are we really in?"

Today's market environment and competition are placing significant pressure on the profession to change. If the facts are ignored and you do not provide your clients with the type of proactive services they want and deserve, then there is a good chance things will blow up in your practice. What I find remarkable is that a preemptive accounting practice is the key to obtaining new clients and maintaining relationships with existing ones, yet so many CPAs continue with the status quo. Although the reward for meeting the preemptive challenge should be obvious—you will earn more money and have more loyal clients—the sad truth is that most of the accounting profession is mentally retired. They define progress as slowly moving backward. You can bet your boots that your competition is going to get much tougher over time as your competitors adjust to these new working conditions.

If accounting firms around the country are making the change to a more proactive, holistic, team-oriented approach to tax and investment planning and are significantly increasing their revenue and profits, why are so many CPAs set in their old ways and ignoring the evidence? I propose that it is not about having enough time, but more importantly, not knowing where to begin and how to do it. What most people need is a blueprint for success and a push in the right direction to offset the tendency to surrender to the pull of the past.

I hope this is one reason you invested a few bucks in my book, as it is my sincere desire that my words will be the nudge to reenergize your practice with a new sense of purpose. I hope to help you transform from a technician working in your company to an innovative business owner working on your company. In today's competitive environment, I suggest that you can't afford to treat your practice as a practice anymore; you have to be an entrepreneur and view it as a business.

I believe that we are in a new era of structural change in the accounting profession, where CPAs have the opportunity to control the bulk of their client's assets. Unlike cyclical changes that we observe in the climate or stock market, a structural change is a deep-reaching change that significantly alters the way things get done. For instance, what structural change killed Kodak? It was the digital camera. What is killing digital cameras? Smartphones. How about Blockbuster video? Netflix and pay-per-view. How about CDs? Yes, iTunes. These are structural changes (no going back) that are taking place because of computers.

As I understand it, a structural change is happening right now with CPA and wealth-management services. Make no mistake; it's coming. Trying to fight structural change often makes us look remarkably stupid. I'm absolutely convinced that the future for the accounting industry will be the incorporation of financial advisory services, in one fashion or another.

The fact that you are reading this book indicates to me that you recognize you need to improve on the service and advice that you provide your clients, which will subsequently grow your business. In addition, I suspect that you are aware of the debatable once-in-a-century phenomenon that is materializing in your profession. I am profoundly convinced that there is an enormous opportunity for CPAs to excel and differentiate themselves as their clients' most trusted advisor.

"I would like to be your trusted advisor. When you want reliable information about drooling, butt sniffing, barking, licking or carpet stains, I'm your man, er, dog!"

The current economic climate provides an exceptional opportunity for you to expand on your traditional services by incorporating asset management into your mix. The evidence is overwhelming that clients want their CPAs to be more involved in the process of helping them make better-informed decisions about their financial future. Clients are more than ever in need of a trusted wealth manager. Who better to be that person than their trusted CPA? If you are like most accountants I know, your clients already look to you to guide them through tax planning and preparation; you know their finances inside and out. Furthermore, they view your services as objective and transparent, without conflict of interest. I suggest that these clients would love you to become their trusted advisor whom they turn to with all their financial and investment needs.

Research has confirmed that the accounting profession is becoming more commoditized by the day, thus creating a need for CPAs to differentiate themselves in the marketplace. I concur with the talking heads that proclaim that the old vision of a CPA serving primarily as a tax and audit professional is an outdated and broken model. During my 28 years as a financial advisor, I have personally witnessed numerous clients swapping CPAs if they can get a better price for tax preparation and auditing. As studies have confirmed, the overwhelming majority of businesses that attempt to compete by being the low-cost provider will die a slow death.

> Fortunately, to take your practice to the next level doesn't require a lot mental power, salesmanship, charisma, a golden tongue, or some incredible business acumen. What it does require is confidence and a burning desire to get it done.

Nevertheless, what I have discovered is that most accountants are in denial of the data. I suggest that accountants who fail to take advantage of the opportunity of offering wealth-management services run the increasingly high risk of going the way of the dinosaur. The essential questions are how to do it and how to do it properly. As with most new ventures, it can be loaded with difficulties. Maybe this is why the vast majority of CPAs have decided to maintain the status quo.

If you happen to be one of those rare breeds who recognize you can do better and you are determined and ready to improve on the services you offer your best clients, I propose that all you may need is, maybe, just a little push in the right direction along with a blueprint for success. If you feel you dropped the ball regarding your dream of becoming the best you can be, I recommend that you put the past behind you and meet the future head on.

I submit that any perceived underachievement has very little to do with you. It is a significant challenge to expand a practice, given the plethora of approaches and misinformation available within the accounting industry on the subject of transitioning to wealth-management services. Furthermore, to my way of thinking, CPAs are in a major state of confusion. They understand a transition of sorts is necessary, but they don't know what steps to take, or in what order to take them. If the abundance of information and techniques has left you more bewildered than empowered, it is time to take a deep breath and relax. I am about to take aim at this confusion, blowing away the smoke, and making things as simple as possible for you.

Fortunately, taking your practice to the next level doesn't require a lot mental power, salesmanship, charisma, a golden tongue, or incredible business acumen. What it does require is confidence and a burning desire to get it done. I believe that committed and forward-thinking CPAs just need some guidance, mentoring, and coaching by the right person with the right message at the right time. Now is that time! The hard part is really just clearing away the smoke, as there actually are no secrets to success. We already have available everything we need to know to make our businesses more profitable without giving up the things that matter most to us.

FAILING LIKE A BUGGY WHIP MAKER

You likely have heard the buggy whip analogy. Buggy whips are a humane device used to make a snapping noise to encourage the horse to move faster. Many people are not aware that the whip never touches the horse. The buggy whip is often cited as an industry that died because it did not adapt to the advent of the automobile. The analogy can be traced to that same 1960 *Harvard Business Review* article in which Theodore Levitt wrote about near-sighted marketing. Today, any line of business facing the life-or-death challenge of a digital age might be characterized as a contemporary buggy whip maker.

Not all horse and buggy suppliers suffered the same fate as the buggy whip manufacturers. A few adapted and innovated. According to Thomas A. Kinney, an assistant professor of history at Bluefield College in Virginia and author of *The Carriage Trade: Making Horse-Drawn Vehicles in America*, there were 13,000 businesses in the wagon and carriage industry in 1890. A company survived not by conceiving of itself as being in the "personal transportation" business but by commanding technological expertise relevant to the automobile, he said. "The people who made the most successful transition were not the carriage makers, but the carriage parts makers."

As we well know, businesses die, even very large ones. In order to protect ourselves from becoming commoditized, we need to know what would cause our clients to ask, "Is there a better, less expensive CPA (financial advisor)?" For those of us who regularly ponder this question, we need to innovate and to improve what we deliver so that our clients would never dream of questioning our advice, services, and price.

Proverbs 29:18—Where there is no vision, the people perish, but he that keepeth the law, happy is he.

I submit that clients hold the key to our success by their willingness to tell us what they want and how to improve. We must ask them, even though they do not always divulge what they really want.

There is an old saying that if Henry Ford had asked his customers what they wanted, they would have told him that they wanted faster horses and more comfortable buggies.

Regardless of your position, my experience has been that the overwhelming majority of clients will clearly articulate their desires for better service. At the end of the day, we must be able to do for the clients what they can't do for themselves. We must focus on the mastery of knowledge that empowers us to solve our client's most pressing issues and concerns. If we don't, we risk becoming the next buggy whip.

The days of paying lip service to being proactive are over. We must go over and beyond what we are trained and expected to do in order to provide our clients with the service and advice that they want and deserve. To most people, accounting is a tedious, routine, unexciting, number-crunching profession. That is what I used to believe. I can say without question that I never met an accountant who performs primarily compliance work who had a real passion for the job. However, for those accountants who work outside the traditional accounting box, it is an entirely different game. Not only is there passion, but also it becomes contagious. Their hearts gets carried away with a purpose far greater than themselves. Things become exhilarating, innovative, fast moving, and extremely rewarding for these forward-thinking CPAs and their clients.

Of course, I don't have all the answers and I am not suggesting under any circumstance that my way is the only way. I am not an accountant, but I have worked closely with accountants for 28 years. I have discovered that most of them are great at accounting, auditing, and tax preparation. Frankly, accountants are so effective at this stuff that I have witnessed them getting so caught up in the accuracy of mumbo jumbo that they don't realize that the information may not be pertinent. Some are so focused on compliance and deadlines that the urgent drowns out the important, which results in lost opportunities to perform more value-added and tactical services.

My work with accountants has revealed to me that few have the necessary knowledge, desire, and experience to operate a business and create real value for their clients, which ultimately is what they need to make their business more profitable. This lack of business experience and confidence to progress up the value chain has kept them from expanding their services beyond tax preparation and auditing.

I find it remarkable that business owners have such a low level of expectation of their CPAs. If you are a forward-thinking CPA, this creates a fantastic opportunity for you to differentiate yourself from your competitors. The highly successful CPA firms continue to offer wealth management as a competitive advantage. In that way, CPAs can deepen their client relationships and provide more and better services to their clients.

THE ODD-COUPLE QUANDARY: WHAT WE THINK BUT ARE AFRAID TO SAY

CPA referrals are viewed as the Holy Grail of new business for financial advisors, yet it is one of the most misunderstood business strategies in our industry. Although it makes perfect sense for advisors to form alliances with CPAs, most advisors fail at creating successful relationships. According to Tiburon Strategic Advisors, in their report *Tiburon Strategic Advisors' Research on CPA Firms: Auditing; Tax and Financial Planning; and Consulting*, 77 percent of CPAs want to form strategic alliances with investment advisors to better serve their clients. So the desire is there, but not the action.

Why has it been a bust? On paper, it appears that CPAs and financial advisors should enjoy a gratifying synergy in which each professional is assisting and improving the other's business development and together they create an impressive experience for their mutual client. This match made in heaven is analogous to the turmoil and conflicts experienced between Oscar and Felix in the legendary TV series *The Odd Couple*.

As a broad observation, CPAs in general are very wary of financial advisors. CPAs have told me that part of their responsibility is to protect their clients from the commission-focused, overcompensated, prima-donna financial advisor. If we flip that around, many financial advisors consider the CPA as a robotic, boring, dull, introverted creature who is void of emotions and who simply enjoy killing deals. Of course, these feelings have not stopped my colleagues from attempting to capitalize on the lucrative CPA network! However, the penetration into this seemingly profitable relationship has been lukewarm at best, as CPAs continue to act like mother hens protecting their young from the foe. The sad part about all of this is that CPAs know deep down that they need a team to support them, but everything they have observed of financial advisors has caused them to be exceedingly guarded.

Proverbs 11:13—Whoever goes about slandering reveals secrets, but he who is trustworthy in spirit keeps a thing covered.

I believe the primary stumbling block keeping this odd couple apart can be explained by the following six issues:

1. **Pay scale**. CPAs have long looked with envy at the sizable commissions/fees that financial advisors and insurance agents are paid for executing a financial plan that the CPA initially masterminded. They

are tired of sweating over tax returns for modest fees while watching financial planners rake in the big bucks. Traditionally, CPAs have been averse to commissions or anything else that implies self-dealing. The fact of the matter is that a lot of resentment exists, considering that the average salary of most CPAs is substantially less than that of financial advisors. Added to that, clients consider the CPA, not the financial advisor, to be their most trusted advisor. I get it! Something doesn't add up!

2. **Work structure**. In stark contrast to the financial service industry, the longer employees are employed by an accounting firm, the more they can expect to work and increase their commitment to their job, especially if they want to become a managing partner. On the other hand, financial advisors tend to pay the price early in their careers with the long hours, but once they have an established business, the hours, typically, decline considerably. CPAs tend to have a salary plus bonus arrangement, while financial advisors typically work for a commission and/or fees. At the end of the day, the two pay structures are miles apart, which can lead to resentment. Let's not forget the laborious 60–80 hour workweeks that accountants put in during the three-month busy time, relying on strong coffee and late-night take-out dinners. While CPAs struggle to stay awake, I can only imagine what they think of their client's financial advisor!

3. **Sales versus consulting paradigm**. We are considered salesmen in the eyes of CPAs, and accountants don't like salespeople. Most CPAs view selling with scorn, and salesmen with mistrust. Even if accountants have sales people working for them, they view selling as something that is beneath them. It's true. As much as I never considered myself a salesman, it quickly became apparent that most CPAs viewed my fellow advisors and me as salespeople trying to earn a commission. To an accountant, we all look like money-grubbers who

want to get into their client's wallets to beef up the bank account. Although there are bad apples in every batch, I can say without reservation that there are many thousands of honest, ethical, knowledgeable, and fee-based financial advisors who help their clients live their dream day in and day out.

4. **Advisors don't get it**: Accountants clearly see the benefits to advisors when they provide referrals, but the benefit to them is less clear. The advisors regularly make the crucial mistake of assuming that CPAs will be motivated by money (revenue-sharing arrangement). I recommend that advisors need to apply the law of reciprocity by giving without expecting anything in return. Do what is right for the client by providing valuable service to the CPA. Most advisors are from the school of entitlement, which asks, "What have you done for me lately?" These folks completely dismiss the law of reciprocity. On the other hand, a value-driven advisor says, "What can I do to help you? I will work diligently and then I hope you recognize my exertion and reward me." In other words, givers consider the needs of others before they think of their own needs.

I hear repeatedly from advisors that they give CPAs referrals and seldom receive any in return. This is an entitlement mindset. A value-driven position puts it this way: Don't worry about sending me referrals. Allow me to work hard for you by creating tremendous value. Only after you get to really know and trust me should you consider engaging our services. Regrettably, the truth is that we live in a society of takers, not givers. "The principle of give and take is the principle of diplomacy; give one and take ten," Mark Twain quipped. Self-interest is hard-wired in our being.

John C. Maxwell, author of *Teamwork 101: What Every Leader Needs to Know*, said, "People who take advantage of others inevitably fail in business and relationships. If you desire to succeed, then live by these four simple words: Add value to others. The philosophy will take you far." Everyone appears to have an agenda, which is usually to get what he can for himself. If financial advisors would simply observe the law of reciprocity while working with CPAs, I honestly believe a major shift in attitude would occur.

5. **Unfamiliarity breeds mistrust.** I submit that the majority of accountants are incredibly uncomfortable with anything that is not black and white. I don't believe CPAs are really familiar with what many of us do for our clients from a comprehensive, fee-based, philosophical approach to investing. In addition, CPAs are often ill informed with respect to the Ritz Carlton-type of service many advisors provide to their clients. Let's assume that the aforementioned four items are spot on. How on earth does the advisor ever get the opportunity to demonstrate to the CPA how they are different and how they can provide considerable value to their practice and clients? This is the real crux of the problem. It is the chicken-and-egg dilemma. Although it should be discouraging for all three parties (CPA, advisor and client), there is hope, particularly as the CPA profession begins to implement The Better Way model of working with financial advisors.

6. **Introvert versus extrovert.** Frequently in business, when an introvert and extrovert collide, the outcome is not good. I am sure it is no surprise that research clearly indicates that most CPAs are introverts, while the majority of financial advisors are extroverts. The Myers & Briggs Foundation, an organization dedicated to the understanding of different personalities, provided a list of six career opportunities in which introverts can excel. As you might imagine, accountants rank number one, while there is no mention of financial advisors:

Career #1: accountant

Career #2: graphic designer

Career #3: medical records and health information technician

Career #4: financial analyst

Career #5: computer programmer

Career #6: technical writer

True confession: I am a hard-core introvert and proud of it! Perhaps like you, I enjoy the company of a good book and a view, and spending time with my wife and kids is far more pleasing to me than a social gathering with friends or colleagues. I exhaust most of my social energy while working. I crave isolation, as this is where I get energized by my thoughts and dreams. I have been told too many times that I am boring. I quickly reply, "I'm not boring at all. I just get excited about boring things." A few years ago, I completed a DISC personality profile that placed me in the high C category: systematic, isolating, analytical, conscientious, valuing quality, and accuracy. I was not aware that I was considered a high C, but I did not require a test to inform me that I was a classic introvert or that I would score well on communication skills. This is how I have been labeled for as long as I can remember. Possibly, like you, I prefer one-on-one interaction with individuals rather than interaction with a large group.

"The Happy Introvert" book.

While I have been around plenty of accountants who had just enough social skills to survive the office holiday celebration, most accountants are not the academic, shy, anxiety-ridden geeks who love pocket calculators, as extroverts might imagine. Meanwhile, not all extroverts are the less-intellectual, insecure, oxygen-sucking, spot-light-dominating, sales-oriented creatures they are often portrayed as being. I suggest that we wipe the slate clean and give both professions the benefit of the doubt. It is easy for us to fall prey to stereotyping introverts and extroverts, but frequently our analysis does not correspond with the facts.

If CPAs and financial advisors are indeed the odd couple, who cares? Can't we just get along? We know opposites regularly attract each other in love and marriage, so why can't it be fruitful between CPAs and financial advisors? If you are interested in an excellent, well-researched, and thought-provoking book regarding this subject, I recommend that you pick up a copy of Susan Cain's *Quiet: The Power of Introverts in a World That Can't Stop Talking.*

Proverbs 31:9—Open your mouth, judge justly;
defend the needy and the poor!

OPEN UP, PLUG IN, AND BECOME ENLIGHTENED

According to Buddhist tradition, the Bodhi tree played an important role in the life of Buddha, who meditated under it and received enlightenment. Prior to being enlightened, Buddha studied with the best teachers of the day, and lived the hard life of an ascetic. Yet he did not feel any closer to the truth. The turning point came when he nearly died of hunger. Shortly thereafter, under the Bodhi tree, Buddha discovered the truth about life.

Enlightened refers to the attainment of a new and unique insight into a specific difficulty. It is my hope that you become enlightened as you discover the truth about the enormous potential for incorporating wealth management into your practice. Nonetheless, trying to encourage you that there is a better way may be exceptionally difficult, especially when we don't know each other. You could be a cynic or know-it-all who enjoys doubting just about everything and everyone. If you are that kind of person who enjoys lobbing sarcastic grenades and poking holes in the dreams and aspirations of others as you cling to the status quo, it will be virtually impossible for me to influence you. You spend your time investing in roadblocks.

AN EARTHLY STORY WITH A HEAVENLY MEANING

I am humbly requesting that you open up your heart and become fertile soil. If you are a Christian, you perhaps know that Jesus is the dominant character in the first four books of the New Testament. Jesus shared tales that have a powerful and significant meaning. You may be familiar with Jesus's story of the farmer who planted seeds in four types of soil. If you have ever planted a flower or vegetable garden, or maintained a lawn, you can quickly comprehend this legendary parable. Jesus is telling us that God is the farmer, his Word is the seed, and the soil is in the hearts of each of us.

1. The first type of soil that Jesus refers to is the kind you would find along a trail where it has been trampled. This soil is so packed down that seeds have virtually no chance of producing results. The person represented by this soil

is someone who has a rigid covering and a callous heart. It is very difficult to motivate this person to do anything.

2. The second type of soil is a thin coating of dirt, but it is surrounded by many rocks. Though the seed grows initially, it soon weakens and dies from lack of moisture. Those who are represented by this soil welcome the Word with excitement and joy when they hear it, but it doesn't take root. They believe and want to change but, over time, revert to their customary habits.

3. The third type of soil Jesus refers to is good soil, but there are so many weeds surrounding the good soil that the plant eventually dies. This type of person has many distractions (weeds) in life that eventually choke out God's Word.

4. Finally, the fourth type is fertile soil that is free of weeds and rocks. With this soil, the seed is able to take root and becomes fruitful and productive. This type of person hears the Word, opens his heart, and retains the information, which ultimately produces a crop.

Commit yourself to staying open. If you don't, you may never discover an epiphany. You purchased this book for a reason. Respect that purpose and stop accepting your present-day business circumstances as the way things have to be. In their place, I want you to think, "breakthrough!" We are going after something more productive and efficient that creates significantly more value for your clients. In the end, you will do more while working less. In order to access a breakthrough, we must look outside the long-established approach of doing business and be responsive to new ideas and possibilities.

I urge you to become fertile soil by having an open mind, instead of being a prisoner of habit. Be receptive to a new method of serving your clients, and it should become clear to you that what I am suggesting could be the beginning of something rare and very special. This new approach should begin to make undeniable sense to you. I hope that my words rouse a sense of excitement in your heart and breathe new life into your business and personal existence that has been long forming. Maybe what I have to say is the missing link that will help take your business to the next level.

Proverbs 1:5—He that is wise will hear, and will increase learning; and the intelligent will gain wise counsels.

CHAPTER 7

Data Dump

I have observed that people genuinely don't want more information. In fact, I think they are already in information overload. Instead, folks are looking for inspiration and motivation where faith becomes the spark that sets things in motion. Providing facts, data, surveys, and so on, doesn't accomplish this in the least.

Nevertheless, I feel compelled to data dump on you. My apologies, but it may be for your own good. The primary purpose of a data dump is the hope that it provides credibility to one's message. According to bestselling author Jerry Weissman, in his outstanding book *Presenting to Win*, this is known as the "Frankenstein Approach," in which disparate body parts are assembled. At the risk of boring you to death, I feel it is necessary to provide you with oodles of compelling data that discuss what the accounting firm of the future will look like. If the following research, data, and statistics mean nothing to those who question the viability of CPAs entering the financial advisory space, I suggest the words of Winston Churchill would be appropriate to open this chapter, "If you don't look facts in the face, they have a way of stabbing you in the back."

Mark P. Hurley published an attention-grabbing report in April 2013 titled *The Brave New World of Wealth Management*. Mark and his team produced the analysis to provide owners of wealth-management businesses with a macroview of the current state of the industry, and given the forces confronting the industry today, how you can expect the structure and economics of the business to evolve over the next decade. Mark suggests that the "easy money from this industry has already been made, and only those organizations that adapt their strategy and business model to the reality of the next decades will prosper. The owner of those firms that cannot adapt will have to work harder for less money and the businesses will ultimately have little enterprise value."

The study recognizes that the wealth-management business is becoming significantly more challenging and that new clients are harder to find. Operating costs and employee compensation, in particular, are increasing and regulators are becoming more hostile. A rapidly changing and increasingly adversarial regulatory environment is likewise forcing, and will continue to force, wealth-management firms to spend more of their time and resources on compliance. Consequently, wealth managers have to spend substantially more money on legal advice and dedicate more management time to compliance issues. Additionally, the compliance function will have to be run by a more qualified and more highly compensated individual than in the past.

I read a jaw-dropping report titled "Intuit 2020: Twenty Trends That Will Shape the Next Decade." The report identifies 20 demographic, social, economic, and technology trends that will shape the next decade, and it emphasizes one particular truth: the disarray we are witnessing today will intensify as the next ten years play out, and CPAs will play a role in bringing order to that chaos. "The world is rapidly becoming more complex," said Steve King, principal researcher for Emergent Research, which conducted the study in partnership with Intuit. "Small businesses in particular are going to need more assistance in understanding this complex world. Tax law changes, health care changes, environmental law changes, globalization, just to name a few—there are a lot of areas in which businesses will need help, and that's a great opportunity for CPAs."

Here is a wonderfully written, entertaining, and provocative article by Frank Stitely in the June 12, 2013 issue of *CPA Trendlines*. Although I categorically agree with Stitely's dispatch, I think that he overlooked what could be the most important trend of all, which is CPAs' entry in the wealth-management space. It's worth noting that Stitely's website gives no mention of providing wealth-management services:

THREE TRENDS THAT WILL TRANSFORM YOUR TAX PRACTICE OR ELIMINATE IT:

"Worst tax season ever."
"The death of the 1040 practice."
"I'm retiring."

Since the end of tax season, CPAs voiced apocalyptic concerns. You can blame this latest meat grinder of a tax season on Congress, competition from TurboTax, and the IRS. Or you can recognize that three trends are converging that will either transform your practice or eliminate it.

Trend 1: Zero Data Entry

Tax practice will no longer be about sitting in a back room entering W-2s and 1099s into a PC. Modern tax practices will tap into existing electronic transactions to capture tax-related data and feed it into our tax software with zero data entry. Scanning documents using OCR software to input W-2 and 1099 data is a meager beginning. If you've used OCR technology with your tax software, you know it's too unreliable to be the answer to zero data entry. Soon, we'll be tapping directly into IRS, bank, and brokerage data to get W-2 and 1099 data. If your primary tax skill is data entry, your career is nearly over. Burger King is hiring. Tax practice in the twentieth-first century is about workflow and quality control. It's about harnessing electronic data, moving it through an efficient process, and ensuring that the results are correct and timely. Either you'll spend a lot more on technology or you'll be out of business. Barriers to enter our profession are becoming higher. The technology of the 1990s mostly eliminated the seasonal, part-time preparer. The practices TurboTax didn't kill were killed by the annual cost of tax software. The part-timers were effectively working for minimum wage after expenses. Those of you who spend the absolute minimum on tax software paid the price this year in buggy software and overstretched technical support. Your choices will be to spend more on better-quality software or disappear. The '90s killed part-timers. The twenty-first century is killing small 1040 practices. Zero data entry will make you step up or step out.

Trend 2: Changing Demographics Change Our Client Relationships

Since the beginning of our profession, we've had parent-child relationships with our clients. We told them what to do and they did it, mostly without question. They recognized us as experts and took our advice without debate. As our clients age and older clients are replaced with younger clients, we face a different attitude. Younger clients reject the parent-child relationship model. They want to be involved in and shape their income tax situations. They view themselves as our peers. They don't view us as infallible experts whose advice must be taken without question. They want more than just tax returns, recitations of the past. They want advice that can change their future circumstances. Help them improve their circumstances, or they'll find a CPA who will. The changing demographics of our client bases also affect how we communicate with clients. The telephone generation is literally dying. Younger clients view telephone calls as unwanted intrusions. In the mall, note the difference in cell phone use between 50-year-olds and 20-year-olds. The 50-year-olds are talking on the phone. The 20-year-olds are texting. Portals and e-mail aren't the future; they're the present for serving younger clients. You can either adopt new communication methods or watch your practice die with your clients.

Trend 3: The CPA Firm as a Business

To see how this trend will change our profession, look at the changes our clients in medicine have endured. You don't have as many doctors as you used to? That's my point. Medicine became a business. Twenty years ago, doctors simply treated patients and earned great incomes. Then insurance companies and Medicare clamped down on costs. As medicine became a business, patient service wasn't the only metric that mattered. Cost containment demanded revolutionary changes that included production and efficiency metrics. If you don't believe the part about metrics, go to www.mgma.com. They'll sell you a subscription. If you serve medical clients, you had better buy one. Medicine became more capital intensive. Solo and small medical practices combined to share overhead, were sold to hospitals or went out of business. We are ten years behind our doctor brethren. Regulatory forces pushed medicine toward efficient business practices. Competitive forces have more slowly pushed our profession toward the same outcome.

As trend one above makes our practices more capital intensive with ever more investment in hardware and software, and the era of the data-entry tax preparer ends, we will need higher-level staff who can thrive in the new era of zero data entry. Those staff will be more expensive and harder to find. No more hiring masses of asses in December and then laying them off in late April with the notion that next December there'll be more asses to hire. Higher-end staff requires ongoing training.

If we invest in these people and then lay them off, they won't be around next year. Our competitors will have them. The end to disposable seasonal staff means a real investment in people. We'll need methods to ensure we get sufficient financial return on that investment. Welcome to the world of professional practice management where costs matter, and welcome to the CPA firm as a real business. These three trends aren't asking for your permission to proceed. You can welcome the changes these trends will bring and thrive. Or, you can join many of your small firm competitors in retirement while your more forward-thinking competitors absorb your clients.

If your firm gets caught behind the curve, it wasn't because critical trends weren't visible; it was because they were ignored. The huge challenge remains that for too many firms, unless there is acute "pain," there is little incentive to change. Are you able to make the leap and recognize the accounting business is no longer the safe environment it has been

> There are fundamentally only two techniques to compete for business. You can compete on price or you can differentiate on value and charge a premium for your services.

for generations? We need to see the competition coming and proactively make the necessary changes in order to thrive. We cannot become the victim of our own shortsightedness. To paraphrase the history adage: Those who do not prepare for change surely will perish from it. When does a firm's strategy change? Usually, only in response to a crisis or because of the initiative of a new managing partner. The goal is not to speculate on what might happen, but to imagine what you could make happen. Many firms are in denial, and the few that aren't move very slowly.

I discovered another noteworthy article written by Edi Osborne, CEO of Mentor Plus, and a top trainer and consultant to the accounting profession for nearly 20 years. She was recently named one of the Top 25 Thought Leaders in Public Accounting and has dedicated the past two decades to helping accounting firms move from being "service" centered to "client" centered. In her April 2012 article in the *Progressive Accountant*, she discussed the concept of CPAs moving from "Trusted Advisor 1.0" to "Trusted Advisor 2.0." Osborne points out that practices and services once deemed as discretionary by CPAs are now no longer optional. Below are just a few of Osborne's must-haves for today's CPAs:

- **Market intelligence**. The ability to assess your firm's ideal client demographic and absolutely understand their needs. Partner with others that address the greater needs of clients. Realize and accept that your client's needs can often be better met by other professionals. Seek out and establish strategic alliances with these organizations and individuals so that you together can develop business acumen without leaving vulnerable deficiencies in your arsenal. In essence, create partnerships with experts who can augment what you already do and leverage these partnerships to provide a stronger service base to your clients.

- **Create standardized delivery systems for new services**. It's about creating systems and relentlessly seeking ways to enhance the methods over time to make you more productive without exhausting more of your time and energy. Rather than offering random acts of consulting that become difficult to leverage, you must become a specialist (or team with specialists) to provide a new standard of competency beyond tax, audit, and accounting work.

- **Raise the strategic IQ of the firm by building a bigger picture.** By bringing your entire firm into your goal, you move from a myriad of individual actions to a team approach with futuristic vision. You create direction and momentum, which results in productivity and less attrition.
- **Be virtual.** Utilize the latest advances in cloud computing and mobile technology ASAP. It is a critical component of growth and progression to "Trusted Advisor 2.0."

As Osborne mentions, the rate of change in the accounting profession is accelerating. No longer is there a question of *if* a firm should offer new services but rather *how* and *what*. The progressive CPAs will meet these latest and changing needs by developing a one-stop, concierge-type practice that creates the ultimate and unique client experience, Osborne states. "Those who make the transition to wealth management and adjust to the current and future needs of the clients will not only serve their clients better, but will significantly outshine their colleagues who continue to resist the inevitable."

Another thought leader in the CPA industry is Richard Muscio, a well-known CPA and industry consultant. Muscio specializes in helping CPAs update their practices in order to best keep up with changing times. His recommendations are geared toward obtaining a higher rate of client retention and growth for CPA firms, and he mentors CPAs in becoming trusted business advisors to better serve their clientele. Muscio speaks frequently on the topics of family governance, professional collaboration, business succession planning, and the CPA firm of the future.

According to Muscio, clients need their CPAs to assist them with making important decisions that look into the future. If the CPA cannot assist in such a manner, then clients are not receiving very much value, if any, from their CPA. Patterns of forward-looking services include business cash flow and profitability planning, business risk mitigation, real-time financial statements, business process attestation, income tax planning, business succession planning, business sustainability, and family wealth transfer planning. Muscio explains that if a CPA firm is not performing these activities, or similar services, that firm is probably a CPA firm of the past. To be relevant in the worldwide economy of the present and the future, CPAs must learn how to move beyond the traditional services of income tax and financial statement preparation.

Muscio lists eight attributes that are paramount if CPAs want their firm to become a firm of the future (Muscio's comments are underlined):

1. **Paperless environment.** The benefits of incorporating paperless systems into today's CPA firms are increasingly obvious. Going paperless is not just about hardware or software. Instead, it is about workflow efficiency, record retention, and office space utilization.

2. **People.** Does the firm have racial and gender diversity in its workforce? Does the firm outsource certain basic functions? Are the firm partners only male? Does the firm use flex time or job sharing?

3. **Work flow.** Does the firm have a clearly articulated process that it uses for project management, or is the firm's process based on "the tyranny of the urgent?"

4. **Technology.** As you well know, advancements in technology have commoditized many of the services both accountants and financial advisors offer for a fee. Often, these types of services and information are given away, while we search for higher-value revenue streams. According to its April 2009 study, Gartner, one of the world's leading information technology research and advisory companies, found that more than 86 percent of CPA firms have yet to integrate a customer relationship management (CRM) program into their organization. Additionally, accountants have watched cheap software, such as QuickBooks and TurboTax, continually hurt the profits of routine work. According to technology marketing expert John Ryan, CPAs have been one of the last professionals to see the value of customer relationship management tools. I don't get it. Client relationships are the lifeblood of any accounting firm and should be maintained in an efficient and organized manner. This is what CRM ensures, plain and simple. I have used a CRM system for the past 25 years and it is not only essential, but it is the backbone of my practice. It is a must-have piece of technology for both accountants and financial advisors. The AICPA published a very informative 13-page white paper, "Selecting the Right CRM Application for Your Firm," which I encourage you to read if you don't utilize CRM technology.

5. **Extreme seasonality**. <u>Do CPAs have time to meet with clients in March and April, and in September and October, or do they disappear into the black hole of their office during those months?</u>

6. **Billing by the hour.** Here is what Rob Nixon, author of the outstanding book *Accounting Practices Don't Add Up! Why They Don't and What To Do About It*, has to say about billing by the hour. Nixon believes that billing by the hour is wrong and unethical. This is what he teaches his clients (who have moved away from time-based billing) to say when they are asked the question how much do you charge per hour? Hold on to your hat!

Just about every accounting firm in the country uses charge rates. Those firms that use them are directly rewarded for how inefficient they are. The longer they take, the more they get. In our view, that is unethical behavior. We don't think that it's fair on you, so we don't use charge rates. Instead, we will give you a fixed price for the work that we undertake. You will receive that price in writing and in advance of us starting. When we get into the work, if we are inefficient, then that's our problem—the price remains the same. If the scope of the work changes as we get into the project, then we will inform you of any price changes. Normally, the price does not change because we spend quality time with you at the outset, to determine the exact scope of the work. Overall, we think this is a fairer way to do business." To emphasize his point, Nixon shares this story: "When my son, Hugh, was 12 he asked if there were some jobs he could do at the office. I told him I needed 1,000 stickers adhered to 1,000 paper bags. He said, "How much will you pay me?" I said 10 cents a unit. "Is that 10 cents for the bag and the sticker?" He asked. Smart kid. "No—10 cents per completed item." On the first morning, he did 200 bags in 3 hours and I gave him $20. He was thrilled. I told him he made about $7 per hour. And then I said, "When you come back next week to finish the remaining 800, do you want to be paid 10 cents per unit, or $7 per hour." As quick as a flash, he said, "10 cents a unit. I'll probably do it faster next week." If a 12-year-old gets it, then what is our problem?

Although Nixon is not a CPA and his business is headquartered in Australia, he has forged a niche as one of the world's foremost authorities on how accounting firms can achieve peak performance. Here is a letter that Nixon suggests CPAs who are bold enough to eliminate the time sheet send to their clients:

Since our firm was started in 1990, we have been using a time multiplied by rate per hour method to determine the price of the work. Nearly every accounting firm worldwide uses this method. We have come to the realization that this method is an archaic method of pricing. It is also a conflict of interest because what it means is we are directly rewarded for how inefficient we are. The longer we take to do the job, the more we get. It is not promoting good customer service or faster completion time. This also means you have no idea how much the job will be until the bill is received. We don't think this is fair on you. As a courtesy to you, we think you deserve to know in advance how much the job will cost and what it entails. As a modern and progressive firm, we have decided to change this old business practice. This means that before every job starts, we will advise you how much it will cost. There will be a written communication that you will need to sign off on. If you are uncertain about the project, the price or the benefits, you will have the opportunity to discuss these with us at the outset. To get the new system up and running, we are clearing out all of the time which we have accumulated to date on your behalf under the old system. Accordingly, please find enclosed an invoice, which brings you up to date. Other than for minor incidentals that we attend to from time to time, this is the last time you will receive such an invoice from us. We are indeed bringing in a bold new era for accountants. We appreciate your business very much and are confident that this new method of pricing will enable us to give you a better service. We look forward to working with you under the new arrangement.

7. **Marketing.** <u>Can your firm differentiate itself from the competition?</u> Are you aware that accounting firms are beginning to hire dedicated marketing and sales people with the sole purpose of generating new business? If you can't articulate your "why me?" you are looking for problems as your competition beefs up its sales force. To compete, we must differentiate or die, or, as business management expert Tom Peters says, "Be distinct or become extinct." There are fundamentally only two techniques to compete for business. You can compete on price or you can differentiate on value and charge a premium for your services. Harry Mills, author of the captivating book *The Rainmaker's Toolkit: Power Strategies*

for Finding, Keeping, and Growing Profitable Clients, says that many professional service firms suffer from marketing deficiency syndrome (MDS). According to Mills, "Marketing Deficiency Syndrome is a disease that can afflict any lethargic, sclerotic, professional service firm. MDS is usually contracted by lead-footed firms that fail to inoculate themselves against market-driven changes caused by globalization, deregulation, and technology change. Sadly, most firms who suffer from MDS continue to practice same-old service marketing (SOS)."

8. **Succession Plan.** Does the CPA firm have a coherent business plan to transfer thought leadership and intellectual capital from the current leading generation to younger generations? Or when your CPA retires, do you have to go find another CPA? To accentuate this point, Todd Stanard, managing principal at Paramus, New Jersey-based Lincoln Financial Advisors, suggests there are similar concerns for financial advisors. For instance, the average age of a financial advisor is in the fifties, and a 2013 study by the research firm Cerulli Associates says that the number of US investment advisers is diminishing. Numbers show there were 1.3 percent, or 4,000, fewer financial advisers in 2011 than in 2010. The figure is expected to decline by another 18,600 over the next five years. Recognizing that there aren't enough experienced financial advisers to satisfy the need, the larger firms such as Merrill Lynch are beginning to train their advisors again. Tyler Cloherty, associate director at Cerulli, says, "The wirehouses are starting to train people again, but it's just not enough to

make up for the number of advisers retiring and leaving the industry."

One final report from Rob Nixon draws a similar conclusion. In June 2010, Nixon published an intriguing report titled *The Future of the Accounting Firm*, in which he presented 12 predictions of the future of the accounting firm. I have highlighted three of his predictions below:

1. **There Will Be Fewer Firms but Larger Firms** - The accounting profession is still a "cottage industry" made up of primarily small businesses. There are somewhere in the vicinity of 1M to 1.5M accounting firms in the world. Only (approximately) 60,000 of those accounting firms have revenues above $3M. The vast majority of firms are 1–3 partners, with an estimated 45 percent of all current partners over 50 years of age. There are too many firms and far too many small sole-practitioner firms. According to industry statistics, approximately 65 percent of all firms employ fewer than five people. There should be half as many firms, yet they should be larger in revenue. Many of the current partners should not be partners. If compliance is to become a commodity, then some accounting firms may not be interested in continuing in their current format. To thrive, accounting firms needs to offer a broad range of services, and as such they need to be of larger size with a broader range of people offering those services.

2. **Clients Will Demand Additional Services** - Clients are getting smarter and more business savvy. They have

fast and inexpensive access to information through the Internet and various industry associations. If they know what an accounting firm can offer, they will start asking for it. After surveying over 7,000 business people, they have told us that they are looking for seven key service offerings over and above compliance:

- Growth: help with growth of revenue and wealth
- Profit: help with understanding and improvement
- Cash flow: help with understanding and managing
- Asset protection: help to protect all assets
- Succession: help with selling part or all of the business at some point
- Tax minimization: help with legally reducing tax payable
- Retirement: help with financial retirement or full retirement

Progressive accounting firms can and should be offering these services. If you do not, another firm will.

3. **A Hub of Business Success** – When I enter the door of the new accounting firm, I want to be met by my "client relationship manager" (CRM) who manages my relationship with the firm. This person will assess my needs and determine which services I need to fulfill my future direction. They will then ask various professionals within the business to do the work necessary. I do not intend to visit division after division and be asked the same or similar questions. The "silo"- and "division"-based model is an ineffective business model. This model does not encourage effective "cross selling" or internal referrals. Rather, it promotes "turf wars," "client hogging," and worst

of all, the clients are not properly served with what they need. The client is a client of the firm—not the individual. The new accounting firm will become a "business success centre" and a hub of business—a delivery platform of like-minded providers.

Rob Nixon is emphatic when he proclaims that clients want their accountants to be more proactive with them. He says that accountants must be proactive and add value to the relationship or run the risk of losing clients: "Accountants need to act more like a proactive business than a reactive practice. It's time to stop practicing. You've been at it long enough—you should be good at it by now. Why do you even use the 'practice' word? It should be banned. You've got a business to run and a client base to lead. If you want to improve the performance of your firm, there are 4 As to remember. You must have Ambition, the right A-team in place, take the right Action and be Accountable so you implement." Clients are telling Nixon that they know CPAs know more than what they offer and they want the CPA to tell them in advance what they need to do to be more effective. The evidence stacks up. Clients want more help. The question you need to ask yourself is whether you are in the position to deliver what they want. If not, you can bet that someone else is.

In January 2013, The Sleeter Group conducted research on small and medium-sized businesses across the USA. The goal of the research was to determine what they desired from their accounting firm. Below are a few examples from this thought-provoking analysis. The diagrams below illustrate services that small businesses are currently receiving from accountants, compared to what they would like to have. Take notice that technology service is not listed in the top six services received by clients, yet it is recorded as a desired one.

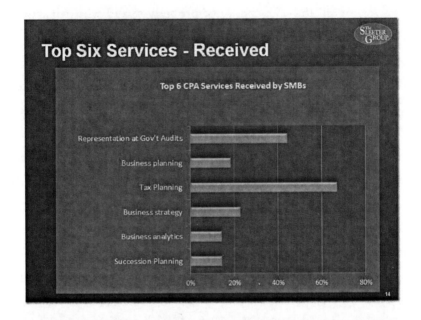

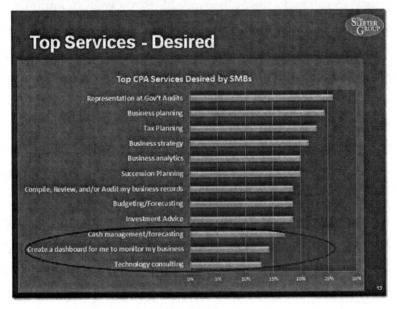

*Proverbs 3:21—My son, do not let wisdom and understanding
out of your sight; preserve sound judgment and discretion.*

I found the following chart to be most telling. Small businesses
have a need for assistance with technology planning, but they
perceive their accountant as either not able or not willing to provide
technology-related planning and consulting services.

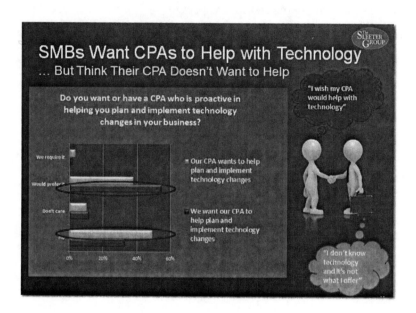

I consider this finding to be an excellent opportunity for accountants to differentiate themselves in the market by providing technology-related services and, subsequently, market themselves as experts
in this increasingly demanded service. For more information on the
survey, please visit www.sleeter.com.

Even with all of the above-mentioned analysis and research, many
CPAs continue to conclude that all of this is just another example
of what my friends in Texas call "big hat, no cows." In other words,
long on talk but short on delivery. I understand and appreciate

the opposing view, but I find it difficult to ignore all the bodies of evidence. Sitting back and hoping that the future does not manifest itself as many believe it will is not a good strategy. In fact, hope is never a good strategy! If you just acquaint yourself with the fact that the AICPA's Personal Financial Planning Section experienced record growth last year, along with the organization's internal studies that showed approximately 100,000 of the 360,000 professionals in the AICPA's general membership are providing financial advice in one form or another. That grabs my attention and makes me sit up and take notice.

CHAPTER 8

Navigating the Maze

One of the trickiest questions facing CPAs turned wealth advisors is exactly how to tap into the financial rewards of a wealth-management practice. There is a justifiable worry concerning the implementation of the correct business model for your wealth-management initiative.

There is no standard model, because the correct approach is what works best for you. Entering the wealth-management business is personal and very individualized. There are many methodologies that have proven successful for a wide variety of CPAs and financial advisors. You must perform your due diligence in order to determine which business approach best meets your goals and objectives.

"We've considered every potential risk except the risks of avoiding all risks."

However, I urge you not to become a victim of paralysis by analysis. Although I consider CPAs as being among the most academically gifted people, I put forward that many fall prey to intellect decision avoidance theory by paying too much attention to details. I am reminded of a cartoon that best exemplifies this notion: A well-educated, middle-aged man, standing before a large crowd, prepares to deliver his acceptance speech for winning the Albert Einstein Award for the world's smartest person. The caption reads, "I know so much that I don't know where to start." I submit that a similar situation is occurring with many CPAs. They know so much but don't know where to begin. I encourage you to remind yourself that it is no longer a question of whether CPAs should consider adding wealth management to their existing practice. Instead, it is a question of what is the right way to get it done.

For certain CPAs, my suggestion is to employ The Better Way platform, which will be discussed in detail shortly. Is this a self-serving recommendation? You bet it is, but I ask you to trust that I am speaking from my heart and not my wallet. If you are like me, you probably get suspicious when someone says, "Trust me."

© Randy Glasbergen
glasbergen.com

"I trusted you right up until the moment you said 'trust me'!"

Jeffrey Gitomer, in his *Little Teal Book of Trust*, writes, "Every time someone says 'trust me,' it's because the other person doesn't trust them! Trust is not a request, trust is earned. Trust is not spoken, trust is a feeling."

I hope that by the time you finish reading this book, the trust dial moved favorably in my direction. In the meantime, it is perfectly understandable for you to be apprehensive about my motives and intentions regarding The Better Way. I clearly recognize that my bias will cast doubt on what follows. Still, I believe with the utmost conviction that my preference is in the best interest of the end user, the CPA, and the financial advisor, given one colossal assumption: You create a professional, strategic, dynamic, and integrated alliance with an ethical, competent, trustworthy, experienced, and client-focused financial advisor. That's a mouthful, but it is of paramount importance.

I could devote an entire book to the various methods, nuances, and complexities of the business models available to CPAs who want to integrate wealth management into their practice. Finding the right platform on which to conduct your advisory business is often a time-consuming and puzzling endeavor. I strongly encourage you to read the enlightening and instructive book from the AICPA titled *A CPA Personal Financial Planning Practice*. Not only does the AICPA discuss the various platforms in its book, but also the entire reading is jam-packed with pertinent information. It is an outstanding source of knowledge for anyone considering wealth-management services. Another worthwhile book is *Planning the Transition: How Accountants Can Thrive as Financial Advisors* by Joseph A. Graziano, CFP, and John Graziano, CPA®, PFS, CFP®. Both books focus more on the do-it-yourself platform compared to cosourcing with a financial advisor. Finally, I suggest that you read *The Lazy CPA's Guide for Adding Financial Services to Your Tax Practice* by Nick Hodges, CPA.

As you might imagine, compliance issues will be a challenge. In fact, the perceived complexities with inevitable compliance matters have prevented many CPAs from getting off first base. The business model you select will define the regulatory environment that you will confront. For example, there are basically two types of advisory services. One consists of brokers/registered representatives (RR), while the other consists of registered investment advisors (RIA). Many advisors are dually registered, meaning they can serve in either capacity. The important thing to know is that both groups are subject to different legal standards.

Brokers/RR are subject to FINRA Conduct Rule 2310(a), which states: "In recommending to a customer the purchase, sale or exchange of any security, a member shall have reasonable grounds for believing that the recommendation is suitable for such customer upon the basis of the facts, if any, disclosed by such customer as to his security holdings and as to his financial situation and needs." On the other hand, the RIAs' code of conduct is much stricter. RIAs are required to act in the best interests of their clients and to disclose all conflicts of interest. CPAs who are registered as an RIA are acting in a fiduciary capacity and are held to a higher standard of honesty and full disclosure.

Mike Patton, president of Integrity Wealth Management, makes an interesting observation in a September 1, 2008, *Investment Advisor* article titled "B/D or RIA? The Case for the Registered Investment Advisor." Referring to the lower standard of conduct among registered reps compared to RIAs, he writes: "What are reasonable grounds? Who's to say what's suitable? What if the advisor has the choice of selling two different products, and Product A pays a slightly higher commission but has higher internal fees as compared to Product B. Both may in fact be suitable, but is Product A in the best interest of the client? This requirement seems to be more subjective and weaker than the legal standard an RIA must meet."

Patton goes on to say, "A person's financial life is extremely important to them and as such, they deserve nothing less than the highest standard of care possible. What if you were faced with major surgery? Which standard of care would you prefer your surgeon be required to adhere to? It's no surprise that RIAs wholeheartedly agree with this while brokers tend to argue the dissenting view."

CHOOSING THE BEST PLATFORM

1. Registered investment advisor (RIA). You operate your own fee-only firm as a portfolio manager or consultant. You would select a firm to perform custodial services. This platform is generally considered to be the freest and most flexible business structure. One may charge fees based on a percentage of assets under management, on an annual basis, on an hourly basis or on a flat fee basis. The RIA method is, historically, the most profitable, but it generally requires the greatest commitment of time and money, not to mention a steep learning curve. Thus, it tends to be a great fit for experienced accountants, with the time, team, and technical ability to implement this type of advisory business. Nevertheless, most financial professionals who decide to establish their own RIA are wise to retain an RIA consultant to help with the regulatory application process, which includes things such as ongoing state and SEC requirements, filing annual reports, updating documents, error and omissions policy, and so on. Adding an in-house wealth-management unit to a CPA practice sounds like a reasonable idea, in theory. In practice, however, it is no small task. Cerulli Associates projects the combined RIA and dually registered (hybrid method) market share to make up 24.7 percent of the advisory industry in 2014, up from 18.6 percent in 2010. According to the report, the wirehouse broker model (Merrill Lynch, Morgan Stanley, UBS, and others) will remain a force, but RIAs seem to have momentum on their side. "The RIA market is the winning market of the current and next decade," says Chip Roame, managing partner at Tiburon Strategic Advisors. "The market benefits from so many trends, including the move to independence, the move to fees, and consumers' focus on fiduciary responsibility."

2. Investment advisor representative (IAR). This is someone who works for an RIA. The choice to become an IAR may be regarded someplace between total independence and limited supervision. An investment advisor representative is an individual who provides investment advice to clients on behalf of an RIA and receives compensation in the form of a fee. An IAR is supervised by the investment advisor firm. This model may be appropriate for a CPA who wants to offer fee-only service and who wants the support of the RIA firm or a broker/dealer RIA such as HDVest and 1st Global. With this approach, the agent is taking advantage of the infrastructure and expertise that the RIA has already developed.

3. **Registered representative (RR).** An RR is an agent of a broker/dealer who is paid commissions on the trades placed through the firm on behalf of customers or fees based on assets under management. An RR is licensed by FINRA (Financial Industry Regulatory Authority). This person is often referred to as a stockbroker, account executive, securities broker, financial advisor or financial consultant. This model may be appropriate for an individual who wants commission-based compensation, along with the option of offering fee-based products. The CPA is subject to the broker/dealer's super-

vision, and can only sell products and conduct business authorized by the broker/dealer. For the fee-only route, with no commissions, a broker/dealer isn't even necessary. Creating or affiliating with an RIA along with a Series 65 license is all that is required.

4. Hybrid Model. The advisors charge fees and may also receive commissions. Hybrid advisors have both securities licenses and an affiliation to a registered investment advisor. Many also obtain insurance licenses. At first, many CPAs cringe at the thought of selling insurance, but it just takes one client who was oversold or underserved by a life agent for them to realize that they could have done a better job themselves. The challenge for the hybrid advisor is the inherent conflict of interest when recommending products that will pay commissions to the advisor. Understand the demographics of your practice is very important when deciding on the best model. For instance, if your clients tend to be less affluent, they may not have the minimum asset size to qualify for fee-only strategies. Your only option, in most cases, would be commission-based solutions. Thus, a broker dealer or hybrid model would be more prudent. The hybrid model has become a very popular option.

5. Referral or solicitor's agreement. In its most basic form, the CPA (solicitor) refers clients to a financial advisor, who then handles the client's investment needs. The CPA receives a portion of the quarterly advisory fee. Neither investment advice nor financial products are provided or sold to clients by the CPA. The RIA, not the CPA firm, has control and responsibility over the management of the client's portfolio, although the CPA, under other requirements, is ultimately responsible for the services. The CPA must provide clients with a separate written disclosure document containing information concerning the solicitation or referral relationship, including the compensation arrangement and other information. Many CPA firms that are not willing to commit fully to a wealth advisor division have set up revenue-sharing arrangements with financial advisors. The accountant then monitors the financial advisor's performance and client satisfaction. The most significant attraction for such arrangements stems from the fact that the advisor's brokerage firm directly handles all the administrative work, leaving virtually nothing for the CPA to do other than to monitor the advisor. Keep in mind that some solicitors must be RIAs in certain states in order to legally receive solicitation fees

Fee-Sharing Example

- Client establishes a $1,000,000 fee-only account.
- Client pays 1 percent annual fee, or $10,000.
- Asset manager receives 50 percent or $5,000, leaving $5,000.
- FA receives $3,750/year.
- CPA receives $1,250/year (net).

Hypothetical Revenue Projection for John H. Doe CPA

Number of Clients	500				
Expected Conversion	25%				
Number of Clients	125				
Average Assets/Client	350,000				
Average Annual Fee	1%				
		Year 1	Year 2	Year 3	Year 4	Year 5
Clients Converted		25	25	25	25	25
Total New Assets		$8,750,000	8,750,000	8,750,000	8,750,000	8,750,000
Avg Annual Fee		1%	1%	1%	1%	1%
Total Annual Fee		87,500	87,500	87,500	87,500	87,500
CPA Payout Rate	25%					
New Revenue to CPA	Year 1	21,875	23625	25515	27556	29,760
	Year 2		21,875	23625	25515	27556
	Year 3			21,875	23,625	25,515
	Year 4				21,875	23625
	Year 5					21,875
Total Annual Revenue w/ 8% Growth		21,875	45,500	71,015	98,572	128,332

For Illustrative Purpose Only

I am pleased to say that the fee-based compensation model has taken hold of the financial planning industry, which, coincidentally, is in the best interest of the client. This pricing structure is often referred to as "fee leverage." As assets grow, the time needed to monitor the account does not necessarily grow proportionately. For instance, management of $1 million in assets for a 1 percent annual fee results in $10,000 per year. But if assets under management grow to $2 million and the fee doubles to $20,000, it is unlikely that twice as much time would be required, making this an enhanced revenue stream for the planner. Of course, leverage cuts both ways. If there were to be a sharp market correction, such as a reprise of the 2008–2009 bear market when stock values plunged 50 percent, asset management fees would decline while inevitably requiring more stringent advisor involvement with the client. Under these circumstances, more work would be required for less compensation. Nevertheless, when planned properly, these joint undertakings can be lucrative for the CPA and financial advisor. More importantly, this arrangement is in the best interest of the end user due to cost effectiveness, full disclosure and transparency.

6. Turnkey asset management program (TAMP). Allows independent financial advisors, typically fiduciaries, to outsource the management of some or all of their clients' assets. With a TAMP, financial advisors gain access to managed account services that allow them to offload time-consuming functions, such as research, portfolio construction, rebalancing, reconciliation, performance reporting, and tax optimization and reporting, which allows them to focus on clients' personal financial needs and concerns. The key advantages for advisors are rapid startup, no upfront costs, built-in compliance, and the ability to utilize sophisticated analytics. These advantages do not come without a cost, as TAMPs typically charge clients from 1 to 1.5 percent, and you charge an additional fee for your services. Regardless of the business model you select, you do not have to go it alone. There are many companies such as Schwab, Fidelity, HDVest, and 1st Global that stand ready to make your transition as painless as possible.

This is obviously an incredibly crucial decision and the best advice is to explore all the options, consult with your mentor, ask the tough questions and proceed with caution. In addition, I strongly suggest that you become a member of the AICPA in general, and the Personal Financial Planning (PFP) Section in particular. I consider the AICPA a must-join organization for all those who are considering integrating wealth-management services into their current practice.

If you are serious about entering the world of wealth management, I enthusiastically encourage you to consider obtaining PFS designation. You may also want to consider the CFP credentials. Having one or both signifies your compelling commitment to improving your services and knowledge. Having a powerful combination of extensive tax expertise, along with comprehensive knowledge of financial planning, is impressive and influential.

Corporate finance theory suggests there is no value to shareholders in a strategy that seeks to diversify the business into products or services for which the company has no competitive advantage. The only reason for a company to enter into a new business would be its ability to achieve and sustain a better performance based on a competitive advantage.

Bingo! This has CPA written all over it. You have a remarkable competitive advantage and substantial opportunities to increase your services and value for your clients by integrating financial services into your existing practice. The rewards to you, as a CPA, of offering investment advisory services are abundant, along with the peace of mind achieved by recognizing that you have your clients' best interest in mind.

The AICPA estimates that an average CPA controls about $100 million of assets for every $1 million in annual billings. If a CPA firm can capture half of its clients' total assets, and earn an annual fee of 50 percent of those assets, the firm's annual billings could increase by 25 percent. Even so, the additional revenue that your practice would generate is only one of many worthy incentives for your CPA firm to enhance its traditional-style accounting model. Other reasons to include an advisory service are that it would:

- strengthen the firm's position as the primary advisor;
- exceed client demands and expectations;
- better position the firm for the future;
- deliver more without materially disrupting the practice (depending on the model selection);
- meet the demand for objective advice;
- provide a one-stop service;
- deliver holistic planning on a continuous basis;
- deepen the relationship with the client;
- increase client loyalty and retention;
- separate the firm from the competition;
- replace seasonal, roller-coaster income with financial stability;
- make attracting new talent easier;
- liberate the firm from the billable hours prison;
- generate higher valuations: CPA firms sell for around 1.5 times the revenue. Wealth-management firms sell for about four times the revenue.

WHY SOME CPAS ARE ON THE SIDELINES

In spite of the enormous opportunity for CPAs, many are reluctant to take the jaunt from tax preparer to financial advisor. As you see from the following diagram, there are just as many reasons why CPAs are reluctant to get into the game. I propose there are four primary culprits for the CPA push-back.

1. **TED (time, expertise, desire)**. CPAs want more time, not more work. Yes, the money is enticing, but the potential reward does not seem meaningful enough, considering their lack of expertise in wealth-management services. Given the time and knowledge necessary to be an effective financial advisor, CPAs have very little incentive and desire to make the jump.

2. **The traditional business model**. As stated earlier, many CPAs have an ethical issue with receiving revenue from clients, other than what they receive for the advice and preparation of the client's taxes. This seems to be a reasonable concern. However, as long as the CPA is being

objective, clients should not object to the CPA offering the additional revenue-generating services. Since CPAs already have a track record with their clients in making recommendations that are in their clients' best interest, why should advising on wealth-management issues be any different?

3. **Regulatory concerns**. Many CPAs do not enter into financial advisory business, because they believe the regulatory issues are too complex and time consuming to navigate. This is a valid concern and one that needs to be addressed carefully with each business model.

4. **Boom and bust scenario**. CPAs have become concerned with the extreme volatility of the stock and bond market, especially given the 2008–2009 debacle and the subsequent calls from upset clients.

I submit that the real truth of the matter is that CPAs are complacent. They have their head buried in the sand doing compliance work while the firms of the future are innovating. Nevertheless, they have plenty of work to keep them busy ... for now!

They are failing to understand that what they are doing is service-centric work and not client-centric work. I believe these CPAs have a very shortsighted perception of what true success will look like in the future. Furthermore, I suggest that the CPAs who are not preparing themselves for the future define their success based on their ability to deliver traditional services, rather than measuring their success based on the success of their clients.

CHAPTER 9

Cracking the Code with The Better Way

THE REFERRAL MODEL IS BROKEN

The challenge for many CPAs is that they do not have the time, expertise, skill set, or desire to successfully integrate wealth-management services into their existing practice. Times are changing quickly as today's affluent business owners and high-net-worth families are increasingly expecting and demanding more from their CPAs. The problem is that that most CPAs cannot effectively or efficiently solve many of the complicated business, wealth, and tax challenges their clients are facing unless they have access to a team of properly trained specialists.

For years, accountants have heard they should embrace the idea of adding financial services to their accounting and tax practice's services. However, most CPA firms are reluctant to add investment services to better serve their clients, because of the costs, the licensing requirements, and the liability issues involved. The obvious choice is to form some type of alliance with an investment advisor and possibly sharing in the fee revenue. Evidence clearly demonstrates that the majority of CPAs reluctantly refer these clients to third-party financial professionals. Although CPAs do not embrace the referral model, what other options do they have? Because their clients desire them to be their go-to-person for all of their needs, I suggest that third-party referrals to financial advisors will soon be replaced by a better way. The old way of doing business is inefficient, and no longer satisfies client's desires.

Lindsey Ferguson, a project manager for the AICPA, wrote a powerful article in the *Journal of Accountancy* in May 2012. Ferguson explained that affluent clients are expecting a lot more from CPAs than ever before, and that CPAs must become trusted business advisors (TBA), and this means they need to change the way they operate. One integral part of becoming a TBA is that CPAs will have to stop referring business to financial advisors, because of the inherent risks and inefficiencies of third-party referrals. According to Alex Sonkin, CEO of the Lombardi Group, "The real inconvenient truth is that the current model upon which advisors, CPAs, specialists, and attorneys attempt to work together is broken, and deep down everybody knows it. The industry's response, specifically from seasoned CPAs, top-performing advisors, and the AICPA has been humbling and overwhelming."

Trying to create value for your clients is virtually impossible via the traditional referral model. It is flawed from the start. The referral model points to someone else and not you. Would it not be better to have your best clients becoming your best marketing company for your firm by pointing others to you and not the referral? Besides the hope of getting referrals from financial advisors, CPAs do not consider financial advisors critical or essential to their practice. When it comes to referring clients to financial advisors, I suggest that it's a lose-lose scenario for CPAs. If the financial advisor performs poorly, then your relationship with your client may be in danger. On the other hand, if the financial advisor provides a meaningful service for your client, then the client is telling the advisor's story, not yours!

You virtually have nothing to gain by referring business to third parties. It will not make you irreplaceable or valuable to your clients. The Better Way advocates that nothing is performed or accomplished for the end user without the CPA being directly or indirectly involved. CPAs who make their client the focal point of the relationship grow their firm organically by having their best clients tell *their* story, not the referral's story. Don't let this subtle difference fool you. This modification is huge and is deeply committed to driving value in the delivery of services.

If all you have is option A (the traditional referral model) and it is highly ineffective, it might be worth the risk to refer business to third parties. However, let's assume there is option B, which gives you access to a team of some of the country's most highly educated and skilled professionals who are completely dedicated to your success with little regard for their own agenda. Your team's primary objectives are for you to become more efficient and more valuable to your best clients, thus becoming more profitable. Moreover, your team facilitates client loyalty, deepens client relationships, creates competitive differentiation, and produces organic growth for your practice by shining the light on you—not themselves—while eliminating the inherent risk of the referral model. It is not about winning the applause; it is about putting you on center stage to receive all the credit for a job well done. The praise and recognition is delivered to you because your team wants your best clients to tell your story, not theirs.

In the end, your team creates true value for your practice by delivering a wonderful, value-driven, world-class experience for your clients and you by providing you with the very best answers and solutions and making you look like a mastermind in the eyes of your most important clients. Finally, your team positions you in the marketplace as a knowledge-selling professional instead of a CPA for hire.

If option B were to exist, would you ever consider option A? The good news is that you don't have to imagine it, because option B does exist; it is The Better Way. Through a network of some of the most effective problem solvers in business, you have immediate access to experts who have built their careers addressing the challenges you face. When you become part of this primary, critical, essential, and dynamic team, you are now part of The Better Way family. It is revolutionary, yet simple. It is life changing.

We live in such an over communicated society with so much information thrown at us that we crave a straightforward, step-by-step process, a step-by-step system for problem solving. We want the information to be broken down in a way that makes sense. We want structure, organization, evidence, strategies, and examples of how something is used. In the end, we want and are willing to pay for a blueprint to success. But it must be the real deal. I can get you to that spot.

WELCOME TO THE BETTER WAY

Let's first spend time examining The Better Way from a macro perspective before going narrow and deep into the details. The Better Way is something completely different when compared to the traditional referral model. At its core, The Better Way is a relationship model that works under the premise of leverage. Do you know of any prominent businesspeople or entrepreneurs who have thrived because they performed everything themselves? Successful people surround themselves with teams. There is no exception to the rule. Even the Lone Ranger had Tonto and Silver on his team. Folks who earn a lot of money usually have two things: control and leverage.

"This really is an innovative approach, but I'm afraid we can't consider it. It's never been done before."

One of the best business books I have read on the collaboration approach to leveraging one's practice is Andrew Sobel's *All for One: 10 Strategies for Building Trusted Client Partnerships*. Sobel suggests that in order to meet the more demanding and price-conscious customer, professional service firms must develop teams of professionals, in which relationship managers are able to mobilize the right people, resources, and ideas—across a multitude of organizational and geographic boundaries—into each and every client relationship. Our goal, Sobel says, should be to build a trusted partnership that adds value, reduces risk, and creates stability for both our clients and our firm. He is a proponent of collaboration, in which an organization creates an all-for-one, client-centered culture where people and ideas easily cross organizational boundaries.

Sobel reminds his readers that "one for all and all for one" was the motto of the inseparable Three Musketeers, members of the king's guard in France. Each put the group's interest ahead of his own and the group always came to the aid of the individual. Isn't this how authentic collaboration should function in order to ultimately bring more value and service to the client?

Sobel's comprehensive guide to building large-scale client relationships suggests that we produce six layers of value for our clients to access. Each of the following six layers is achieved through The Better Way approach:

1. **Relationship leverage** occurs when you add value through the relationship experience by creating multiple points of contact. The emphasis here is on earning your clients' trust so they are more easily persuaded to act on your recommendations.

2. **Organizational leverage** refers to adding value by drawing on different capabilities from across the firm. In a sense, you act as an information manager to connect your clients with the right resources at the right time.

3. **Network leverage** refers to a focus on external connections that you can use to benefit your clients. I also refer to this as connection value.

4. **Market leverage** simply means bringing your clients interesting, useful, and up-to-date information about their competition, their customers, and the market within which they operate.

5. **Innovation leverage** refers to clients' need for more new ideas and perspectives from their advisors. The ability to generate insights for clients is an increasingly fundamental

capability that separates the market leaders from the average firms.

6. **Technology leverage** means using technology to improve communication with clients. In other words, make it easier for the clients to do business with you.

The Better Way experience should absolutely change the lives of CPAs who are ready for it. It's not magical, it's logical, but it supports an unusual order of logic that most people don't recognize. It's about common sense and simple mechanics wrapped into meaningful relationships.

I am not preaching any type of get-rich-quick scheme to you. I'm talking about a way of conducting business that is built on the foundation of ethics, integrity, and doing what is in the best interest of the end user (your client). This is on purpose, with passion and by design, because it operates under the premise of what a wise man told me a long time ago, "No wealth or success can withstand, unless it is built upon truth and ethics." Although The Better Way was challenging to build, it is simple to operate and the results are often immediate.

Keep in mind that I said it was simple. I didn't say it was easy. One must be willing to initially invest the time to reap the rewards in the future. One of the many reasons The Better Way is attractive to many CPAs is that there is no capital required to integrate the system into an existing practice. If you are like other CPAs, once you expose yourself to this business model, you should never want to entertain a referral relationship with a financial advisor again.

> The Better Way experience should absolutely change the lives of CPAs who are ready for it. It's not magical; it's logical, but it supports an unusual order of logic that most people don't recognize.

MORE TIME = FREEDOM

When you established your CPA practice, I am sure it wasn't your intention to work 50, 60, or 70 hours per week, possibly sacrificing the things that matter the most to you. Like most people, you want to be as successful as possible but not to the point where you can't enjoy your success. The word *success* normally signifies making a lot of money, but for me, it's not about money; it's about having more time, which means freedom to be able to do what I want, when I want.

My work is not a job. It doesn't own me. I own it and that is on purpose and by design. I own an enterprise that produces time, which gives me my freedom. I have the freedom to travel, freedom to enjoy my family, freedom from alarm clocks, freedom from the pressures of money, freedom from bosses, and freedom to passionately pursue my dreams. As Michael E. Gerber says, "The entrepreneur creates an enterprise. The technician creates a job."

I submit that just about every successful businessperson struggles with work-life balance. Mike Michalowicz, author of the *The Toilet Paper Entrepreneur*, has said that the final words of Sam Walton, the founder of Wal-Mart and one of the world's richest men, were simply "I blew it." As he lay dying, surrounded by his family, he had never had the time to rightly enjoy the fruits of his labor. One of the richest, most successful men in the world knew that he had done things wrong. There were no destinations on Sam Walton's train and, more importantly, he never enjoyed the ride. He was on a nonstop journey without a destination, and he paid a dear price for it. He failed, as so many of us do, because he didn't recognize that life is all about the adventure and savoring the moments along the way. As it is often said, nobody ever lies on his deathbed and wishes he had made an extra dollar. It was never my intention to make money in order to acquire material possessions. I prefer to have the four Fs: faith, family, fitness, and freedom.

It seems that the higher we advance in our careers, the greater is the demand for our time. Conventional wisdom says that the more we work, the better the opportunity for success. Therefore, as we progress through our careers, we work harder and harder. It doesn't have to be this way. I suggest that the secret to growing one's business is utilizing leverage, which means doing more by working less. In his exceptional book *True Professionalism: The Courage to Care about Your People, Your Clients, and Your Career*, David Maiser, the world-renowned author of books for professional services firms, puts it this way, "To say you made more money by working more is not evidence of immense intellectual creativity. In fact, I call it the donkey strategy—achieving more by pulling a heavier load! ... but I'll never puff my chest up with pride and say, "Look at me—I'm a donkey: I made money by working more!" As an alternative, we must work more efficiently, not harder. Using the leverage of time and other people is the most fundamental strategy for success. Building effective systems for leveraging other people's time is the path to accomplish more while working less.

The Better Way does this for you. It provides remarkable leverage in order for you to have more time to enjoy the things that are most central in your life. As J. Paul Getty said, "I would rather earn 1 percent on the efforts of 100 people than 100 percent on my own efforts." As we clearly know, there are only so many hours in a day for work. If we merely use our own time, we can only achieve so much. However, if we leverage other people's time, we can increase productivity to an extraordinary extent.

Sam Carpenter, author of the superb book *Work the System: The Simple Mechanics of Making More and Working Less*, explains what he means by working the system:

> Instead of seeing yourself as an internal component of circumstances, enmeshed within the day's swirling events, your vantage point is outside and slightly elevated from those events ... You are an observer looking down on your world, examining the comings and goings of the day as if they are tangible physical objects. Things are simple and now understandable. Step-by-step, one thing leads to another, as the systems around you continuously execute. You constantly work on those systems. You make them better, one by one. Over time, complexity and confusion decrease to be replaced by ordered calm and rock-solid self-confidence. There is little fire killing and no confusion, and as you peer down at your handiwork, you feel an intense self-respect and you are proud of what you've accomplished ... avoid being a worker, and instead be a project engineer. It really is this simple: avoid becoming caught up in the work. Instead, step outside, look down, and isolate individual systems.

THE POWER OF YOUR HUMBLE HUB

Instead of putting all of the weight on their own shoulders by trying to be everything to everybody, forward-thinking CPAs work under The Better Way system by utilizing their team of specialists (knowledge hub) that serves as an extension of their office. They

know that having access to knowledge others do not have is powerful. This knowledge becomes intellectual capital when it is organized in an efficient and productive manner to make it easily shared and deployed, bringing value to the end user.

With your knowledge hub, you control knowledge from one central location. Your hub is all you need, because it has access to the people who have the very best solutions for your very best clients. This is why your knowledge hub enhances your value and relationship with your clients, while simultaneously differentiating you from competitors in your industry. This enables you to cement your role as your client's most trusted business advisor and to expand your practice by offering high-end comprehensive support and solutions to your best clients. Consequently, with The Better Way approach, you will do more while doing less! This novel approach has allowed CPAs to make the money they always dreamed of while having more time to enjoy the things they love.

Yes, there is a better way, one that pools the talents and strength of several professionals and focuses on creating and nurturing relationships in order to become critical, essential, and irreplaceable to your clients. The Better Way is a proven model that offers an irresistible value proposition designed to provide your clients with a world-class experience and to distinguish you from your rivals. The Better Way has rewritten the rules regarding the vital link between CPAs and financial advisors.

The Better Way provides a clear roadmap to success and most of all, it gives us hope. It puts the wind at our sails. "And that's the way it is," to quote the legendary newsman Walter Cronkite, who closed his nightly broadcast with these iconic words, which gave his audiences the impression that they had just seen and heard everything they needed to know. I suggest the same applies to The Better Way.

The Better Way epitomizes humility. I faithfully believe that bona fide greatness comes from elevating others. The Better Way's attention to detail helps ensure that your best clients will be boasting about you (telling your story) and not that of a third-party referral. This is how organic growth within your company materializes. Your world-class team (knowledge hub) works with you and through you. You receive the credit from your clients, while your humble hub works behind the scenes in a client-centered collaborative culture.

This working environment increases your firm's brain trust, which empowers you to provide better service to your best clients. You have a team working together with the one vision, one plan, and one shared passion to achieve success. It is often said, "It is amazing what you can accomplish if you don't care who gets the credit."

Speaking of humility, Winston Churchill was once asked, "Doesn't it thrill you to know that every time you make a speech, the hall is packed to overflowing?" "It's quite flattering," he replied. "But whenever I feel that way, I always remember that if instead of making a political speech I was being hanged, the crowd would be twice as big."

There is arguably nothing more powerful than a third-party endorsement. This is what we do via The Better Way. We endorse you repeatedly to your clients by informing them just how special you are and why they are fortunate to have you as their trusted business advisor. We explain that you are virtually the only person they will ever need to solve their tax and financial problems. We let your clients know from the start that they have access to some of the brightest and most forward-thinking experts in the country because of you, their CPA. We explain the amount of time and work that you put forth to become part of a team of like-minded advisors whose goal is to serve the client. Furthermore, we let your client know that you conduct your business this way because you care about them and that, hopefully, they will see the incredible value that you provide and will be likely to refer others to you. We express to your clients that your goal is excellence—their excellence!

Below is an example of how The Better Way elevates you when speaking with your clients:

> Mr. Jones, I feel compelled to say something in front of John (you), as I consider him to be a remarkable and concerned CPA. As you probably know, John is much more than just a tax guy. In fact, I refer to someone like John as a comprehensive, holistic solution provider for his best clients. John recog-

nizes that it is virtually impossible to provide, in-house, all of the answers and solutions for his client's questions and concerns. To provide his clients the best possible service, John integrated his back office to incorporate a "knowledge hub," where he works with a team of some of the country's very best solution providers to provide unparalleled service for his best clients. He does this because he genuinely cares about you and appreciates your wonderful relationship. There are only a handful of CPAs who employ this knowledge hub concept. I don't know if you are aware of what is involved behind the scenes to solve a situation like yours. This process has taken us about two weeks and numerous meetings and phone calls just to get to this place. John knew exactly what you needed and directed his team every step of the way. John is a very bright and client-focused CPA who is delivering to you today what we consider an amazing solution for you. I applaud John for a job well done and for you to be smart enough to engage such a competent and caring CPA.

COMPETE WITH THE BIG BOYS

Did you know that the top ten accounting firms now provide about 50 percent of the world's accounting services? That may not sound very encouraging, but the good news is that your accounting firm is as large as the largest accounting firm when you operate The Better Way. We provide smaller, independently owned CPA firms with everything they need to compete with the big boys.

My conviction is that the most efficient and practical form of structure for CPA firms is to utilize knowledge hubs akin to The Better Way. If you are not part of this type of arrangement, then there is an excellent chance that you will be competing against one.

In *The Firm of the Future*, Paul Dunn and Ronald J. Baker epitomize what the knowledge hub of The Better Way provides to the CPA:

> More companies are realizing that it is knowledge and ideas that create wealth, not tangible things like real estate and oil. We live in a world dominated by *mind*, not *matter*. Most of these knowledge companies now have a chief knowledge officer whose job is to make sure the company knows what it knows— that is, can access the deep reservoirs of knowledge that exist within the firm in order to leverage it to create even more wealth for their customers. There is a wealth of intellectual capital waiting to be tapped into from these companies by the willing student.

Andrew Carnegie once said: "You can take away our factories, take away our trade, our avenues of transportation, and our money—leave us nothing but our organization—and in four years, we would reestablish ourselves." The principle holds true for a professional service firm. Our intellectual capital is our source of wealth. Instead of billing by the hour (labor for hire), you now are selling knowledge and your clients know how much your fee will be before the work commences. As David Maister noted, "What you do with your chargeable time will determine your income; what you do with your non-chargeable time will determine your future." It is the intellectual capital that is generating the wealth, not the means of producing it.

This is the premise under which The Better Way operates. Expertise is not a commodity and innovation has proven to be an outstanding protection against margin squeeze. When you innovate by employing The Better Way, you will have no true competitor because no one has what you have. Speaking of intellectual capital, a teacher once asked Yogi Berra, "Don't you know anything?" Yogi replied, "I don't even suspect anything."

An intriguing example of the power of intellectual capital comes from Napoleon Hill's *Think and Grow Rich*. The author tells the story of the unschooled Henry Ford. Since Ford only advanced to sixth grade, he was considered by many to be illiterate. The lack of education did not stop Ford from becoming one of the richest men in the world. In fact, many suggest that it actually motivated him to succeed. The story is told about Ford's libel suit against a Chicago newspaper for labeling him an ignorant pacifist. While on the stand, Ford was attacked with questions that the defense attorney hoped would prove Ford's ignorance. Here are this guru's precise words:

> After becoming agitated with the offensive questions, Ford pointed at the questioning attorney, and said, "Let me remind you that I have a row of electric push buttons on my desk and by pushing the right button, I can summon to my aid men who can answer any question I desire to ask concerning the business to which I'm devoting most of my effort. Now, will you kindly tell me why I should clutter up my mind with general knowledge for the purpose of being

able to answer questions when I have men around me who can supply any knowledge I require?"

Back in that day, the knowledge hub was referred to as a "mastermind group." Henry Ford's mastermind group consisted of a group who included Thomas Edison, Harvey Firestone, and Luther Burbank. With your knowledge hub, you too will surround yourself with some of the most forward-thinking financial professionals in the country who specialize in specific areas such as multiple-entity planning, split-funded qualified plans, traditional defined benefit, defined contribution, profit sharing, 401(k) and self-directed IRA plans, Section 79 plans, nonqualified deferred compensation plans, advanced cost segregation, asset protection, alternative qualified solutions, premium finance strategies, ESOP, captive insurance company, traditional long-term-care insurance, corporate disability insurance (buy-sell), asset valuation, professionally managed money, lifetime income solution, charitable lead annuity trusts (CLAT), 1031 exchange platform, and more. We put these arrows in your quiver and your hub becomes your firm's intellectual capital, and together everyone achieves more. It is those with the precise knowledge and systems in place who are able to produce tremendous value for their clients, and in turn, create significant wealth for themselves.

*Proverbs 15:22—Without counsel, plans fail,
but with many advisors, they succeed.*

While the advantages of an ensemble practice are accepted by most, the process of building and managing intellectual capital (the knowledge hub) is difficult and time consuming. Frankly, it is like herding cats, each with its own agenda—at first. Most of these professionals have never worked in a *team* to serve a client. Instead, they have performed as a *group*.

There is a big difference between a group and a team. A group doesn't necessarily constitute a team, because a team requires a coordinated effort. A team is more specialized, in that it includes common resources and collective effort. Teams need members with specialized roles in order to help achieve a common goal. Teams do not come together and develop on their own. They require leadership and cooperation. Groups, on the other hand, are often comprised of people with similar abilities and goals and may not have participating members with different skill sets. Groups come together more casually and will, typically, have less structured meetings than teams.

A successful business needs both groups and teams in order to function effectively. Groups may meet to solve less-complex issues, while teams will be structured to solve more difficult issues. Here is an excellent example of the difference between a team and a group: A group of people gets on an elevator. A team forms when the elevator gets stuck! At the end of the day, does it really matter if we use the term group or team? Only if you want people to figure out how to get out of the elevator!

Proverbs 24:6—For by wise guidance you can wage your war,
and in abundance of counselors there is victory.

The process of organizing a knowledge hub in which team members share a common vision is similar to bringing together the architects, electricians, plumbers, stonemasons, and other contractors to build a home. While the work on the front end is extensive, the dividends it pays on the back end are tremendous and well worth the effort for all parties involved. In the final analysis, knowledge management is about efficiently linking intelligent and caring people to serve clients.

By way of another example, the similarities between an orchestra and The Better Way go deep. The audience (clients) sits back and enjoys the music, but, in the pit, a lot is going on to make the performance perfect. The conductor (financial advisor) is responsible for all aspects of managing the orchestra and is ultimately accountable for the success of the orchestra. The majority of the conductor's (advisor) work is done before the show, where he inspires, leads, organizes, communicates and builds his team (musicians). The conductor and his musicians are in hidden in the pit and away from the audience. They are not interested in adoration or recognition. Instead, they remain behind the scene, while all credit goes to the performers on stage.

Your knowledge hub consists of people seamlessly orchestrating successful outcomes behind the scenes. Not only is it difficult to manage and organize this collective brainpower but it takes expertise to deploy it effectively. But when completed, you will have a well-oiled machine ready to deliver an exceptional experience to your clients.

An excellent example of an organized and efficient knowledge hub in action is how Federal Express delivers a package from, say, Jacksonville to Moscow. The package must first go to the company's knowledge hub in Memphis, where the specialists perform their magic behind the scenes to make sure the package arrives in Moscow the following day. The successful results are due to knowledge and collaboration. This is also the DNA of The Better Way.

YES YOU CAN! YES YOU DO!

According to one of our industry's most respected consultants, Leo Pusateri, "Clients crave clarity and simplicity in choosing a financial services partner. Few get it. Clients will favor those firms and individuals who 'get' just how hard it is to select the right partner, given the overwhelming number of options. To clients, you all talk the same and sound the same." If there is one book that you should add to your self-improvement library, it is Leo's book titled *You Are the Value: Define Your Worth, Differentiate Your CPA Firm, Own Your Market.*

With The Better Way, you have a simple story to tell your clients, "Yes we can! Yes we do!" With your knowledge hub at your disposal, you have virtually unlimited access to the very best solutions regarding your client's tax or wealth planning questions/concerns. This is how you separate yourself from your competition. When you truly understand and appreciate the efficiency of The Better Way along with the power and leverage you have with your knowledge hub, your working conditions take on an entirely new perspective. You stand with your shoulders back and you become excited to tell your story because you recognize that you are different. You understand and appreciate that you are indeed the best game in town.

I don't have to tell you that CPAs are overwhelmed trying to service not only their best clients but their B and C clients as well. In most circumstances, these B and C clients are not profitable and consume a significant amount of the CPA's time. Additionally, in many situations, CPAs are not equipped or trained to solve the more-complex challenges of their best clients. Although CPAs have been well trained in tax preparation, many are not as competent in tax mitigation strategies. Yet clients assume that when they receive their completed tax returns from their CPA, every tax mitigation strategy has been explored to arrive at the lowest tax possible. As most CPAs would agree, this is often not the case.

The Better Way empowers you to think big when it comes to solving your best client's challenges, by working under the assumption that great advisors think outside the box when serving their clients. Clients want and expect their CPA to provide creative forward-thinking solutions that may solve their tax and financial planning issues. By creating a whole that is greater than the sum of its parts, you have the capacity and confidence to say yes when your clients ask, "Can you ...?" "Yes, we can; yes, we do." You then give your knowledge hub a call and say, "You'd better!"

ANATOMY OF A CASE: CONNECT, COLLABORATE, AND COMMIT

The Better Way employs a proprietary ten-step process designed and optimized with the goal of delivering a world-class experience to your clients and you. This proprietary process has three objectives:

1. To solve each client "fact pattern" to the fullest and deliver the very best solution(s);

2. To make you look the best in the eyes of your client;

3. To deliver a world-class experience to both you and your clients.

As the project engineer of The Better Way, you accept a challenge (fact pattern) from your client and turn it over (connect) to your knowledge hub, which I call your rapid-response team. These specialists collaborate to develop and provide you with the solution(s) to address your client's problem (commit). When you honestly internalize and apply your new client service model, your business will never be the same again. It is incredibly satisfying to have control, while knowing your clients are receiving the best possible advice and service.

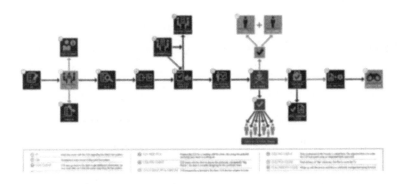

The Better Way's seamless integration into your practice simplifies your back-office operations, enabling you to become the go-to person who delivers the very best service possible to your clients in a timely and efficient manner. With the help of your BOSS (back office solution system), you can solve more of your clients' problems, handle more of their situations, and bring more value to your existing trusted-advisor/client relationship. I am not suggesting just ordinary value, but top value, the very best value, the highest possible value.

This will allow you to do far more for your client than you otherwise could. The Better Way does the heavy lifting for you and nothing is left to guesswork. We have the proficiency to create, generate, and disseminate intellectual capital in order to elevate you to where the air is rare. As with every element of our business, a well-thought-out model and superior execution is key to our success. Every step taken with The Better Way is taken with the CPA in mind.

I encourage you to spend a few minutes listening to an April 7, 2013, interview titled "How Analytics Moves the Business World." Alex Sonkin, CEO of Lombardi Group, is interviewed by Richard Muscio, CPA, and Joe Vecchio on *It's Your Money; It's Your Life*, a wealth-management talk show on 760 KFMB in San Diego, California. The interview begins at the 8:40 mark of the show (www. iymoney.com).

Richard Muscio, CPA & Joe Vecchio

PROACTIVE VERSUS REACTIVE

Today's clients expect and appreciate real value that is measurable, but not measurable in terms of the amount of time spent on completing a project. I say with great confidence that too many accountants and financial advisors are reactive instead of proactive. In other words, they wait for something to happen and then they move into action. They simply deal with what is presented to them instead of making proactive efforts to improve a client's situation. Time is running out. We are in the fourth quarter of the reactive method, as research clearly illustrates that clients want their CPAs and advisors to be more proactive and are demanding a higher level of interaction.

However, most of the accounting and financial service profession is not giving clients what they really want and need. For example, a recent Telberg survey found that more than one-third (35 percent) of clients indicated that the primary reason for changing their CPA firm was because their CPA was not proactive enough. Additionally, a

CPA Trendlines survey indicated that 40 percent of clients gave "They might not be proactive enough" as a reason for firing their CPA firm.

A recent survey by SAGE, a leading solution provider for the accounting profession, revealed that 39 percent of small business owners want their accountants to utilize technology more effectively in order to stay in contact. The Pulse Survey 2013 was undertaken to explore the relationship between accountants and their clients, and almost four in ten people surveyed stated that they wanted to be able to contact their accountants whenever they felt it was necessary, using many of the technological innovations we now have access to. Twenty-eight percent of the people surveyed by SAGE also stated that they would prefer more regular communications from their accountant, whether by phone or by e-mail. These statistics are indicative of a trend in accounting: Clients want to stay fully informed of the financial status of their business at all times.

According to a CCH survey, "It is clear that clients' financial pictures are becoming more complex, with ever-increasing opportunities and pitfalls, and they know they need more help. It is also safe to say that most don't know about the range of services their firm provides. A recent survey found that 70 percent of buyers of accounting services were not aware of all the services their firm offered, and 80 percent said they wished their firm offered services that were in fact already available from that firm." (Hinge Incorporated, 2009). Informing current clients of the full range of services the firm offers and providing more of those services to them is a winning proposition that will improve both profitability and retention for firms as well as benefit clients.

In today's competitive environment, it should be paramount that CPAs discover innovative services and solutions to provide to their clients. I pity those who think they can continue to offer the same services year after year and effectively compete in today's global and technology-driven marketplace. I suggest that if you continue with the SOS (same old service) approach, then you will find yourself in an unfortunate situation in terms of client loyalty, dwindling margins, and ultimately, the demise of your business. The best of the breed are always seeking improvements that produce a competitive advantage for themselves and their clients. If you are providing your best clients with just what they want and nothing more, it would be easy for your clients to replace you. They could simply look for a lower-cost provider. On the other hand, if you provide your clients with more than just their wants, wouldn't that create value to them? Clients know what they know, but they don't know what they don't know. This is a critical point. Why not provide your clients with solutions to problems they did not know existed or ones they did not consider solvable?

As you know, one of the many debates in the accounting profession involves invoicing for time. I am in the camp that advocates billing on the value that you provide. This is what The Better Way empowers you to do. Your clients will recognize and appreciate the value that you offer and be willing to pay accordingly. The Oracle of Omaha, Warren Buffett, said, "Price is what you pay; value is what you get." Of course, it is still necessary and crucial for CPAs to provide basic tax and accounting services in order to remain competitive. However, unless CPAs increase their clients' business efficiency and profitability, they will eventually lose these clients to someone who does. Although I believe accountants know and understand that adding more value (services) is the answer, most continue to turn a blind eye.

Proverbs 21:25—The desire of the sluggard kills him,
for his hands refuse to labor.

By being an innovative and proactive accountant, your clients will unquestionably view you differently. You will no longer be a commodity. Instead, you are a valued and irreplaceable go-to person who provides insight and foresight, and not just hindsight. You will no longer rely on just preparing taxes or performing audit work. You will now actively address the diverse planning needs and wants of your clients because you accept the evidence that plainly demonstrates that your clients want you to take the lead and become more hands-on in anticipating their needs and to providing solutions to their challenges.

Our clients want ideas and suggestions. They want issues dealt with before they become a problem. Ron Nixon says the following about being a commodity, "If you are focusing on what clients think they want (cost), then they can get rid of you. If you are really helping them improve their condition (profit), they can't get enough of you."

It has been my experience that CPAs are not proactive enough in saving clients tax dollars. During my 28 years as a financial advisor, I can count on one hand how many times a CPA suggested a tax reduction strategy for me or my clients. When a CPA did suggest one, it was, typically, a rather minor recommendation, such as a deductible IRA. I think that accountants look at their client's situation through the lens of the services they provide instead of thinking outside the box. In the end, far too many CPAs simply complete the tax return and send a bill. I recognize that identifying how you can help your clients isn't always easy. In fact, many times, clients themselves don't know what help they need. All too often, we think we know what our clients want, but this frequently differs from what our clients actually need or desire. To answer this question from a macroperspective, I suggest that we follow Jeffrey Gitomer's advice in his *Little Teal Book of Trust*, in which he discusses elements regarding what our clients want. If we deliver on the suggestions from Gitomer, how could we possibly disappoint our clients? Here they are:

1. Relate to me. Know my needs and issues.

2. Engage me by showing me other customers who are benefiting from doing business with you.

3. Prepare for me. Show me that you have done your homework about my situation, not just yours.

4. Don't waste my time. Don't ask me what you could have found out on your own.

5. Tell me the truth. Truth leads to trust.

6. Tell me how I can use your product or service to build my business. I want to know how I can produce in my environment.

7. Tell me how I can profit from the relationship. I want to know how I can profit from buying, and I want to know that you know.

8. Show me the value, not just how it works. What are the elements of value attached to your product or services that relates to me?

9. Make it easy for me to do business with you.

10. Make service available when I need it.

11. Next, be friendly to me, if I'm going to establish a relationship with you, I want it to be a friendly one.

12. Respond quickly. If I call you, it's because I need you, and I need a response now.

13. Deliver on time. When you tell me it's going to be there, I expect it, and timeliness reinforces my trust that you can meet my expectations.

14. Have answers for me when I need them. I have questions about how your product works.

15. Stay in touch with me, keep me informed on a proactive basis, and make your message more about me than you.

16. Let me know when things or technology have changed. Keep me informed about how I can stay ahead, even if it means buying more.

17. Keep your promises. If you tell me something will happen, make it happen.

18. Be a partner, not a vendor. Tell me how we will work together. And then prove it by your deeds.

19. Serve me. I need to feel that service after the sale is more important than the emotion leading up to the order.

Gitomer's website is www.gitomer.com. If you are interested in Jeffrey's entire trusted advisor course online, check out www. gitomerVT.com

I know what you might be thinking: where am I going to get the time to do all this work? This is where The Better Way delivers in a big way. We have developed a proprietary, step-by-step, systematic process in which we do all the heavy lifting for you. However, it is imperative that you believe, without question, the following:

1. Your proactive diagnostic process for each client is mandatory. Service excellence cannot be optional.

2. You have a responsibility to your clients to provide this level of service. You guide. The client decides.

3. Your additional revenue earned will more than offset the cost (time) for implementing your proactive diagnostic initiative.

INTEGRATION THROUGH EDUCATION

The integration of The Better Way is a 14-step proprietary process developed by Anthony Lombardi. To become a strategic, dynamic, and integrated team, we adhere to the formula: $(T+V) + (I+A) = S$.

T = Trust: We must earn your trust, grow your trust, and keep your trust.

V = Value: We must provide value to become your most primary, critical, and essential business relationship.

I = Integration: We put our arrows (hub specialist) in your quiver and train you how to be more efficient. What is ours is yours.

A = Application: Two firms working together toward a common goal, delivering an integrated solution to your very best clients.

S = Success: Your success becomes our success and vice versa.

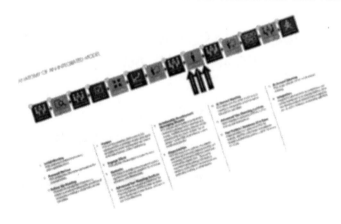

An essential component to The Better Way is the "education through integration" phase. We want you to experience the power of full engagement. We are with you on your journey to building your firm of the future. We don't dump and run. We are your partner throughout the entire process so that you truly benefit from our experience and expertise. Your education in the mechanics of The Better Way is paramount to the successful development of a strategic, dynamic, and integrated relationship. We train and empower you to transition from providing primarily reactive work to becoming proactive. This will position your practice for the future so that you can attract and retain your ideal clients, which, in turn, ultimately differentiates you from the marketplace. During the multifaceted education phase, we optimize your operation by delivering ongoing training and consulting services to you and your firm through workshops, webinars, and our semiannual Advanced Wealth and Tax Planning Conference (AWTPC).

Proverbs 9:9—Give instruction to a wise man, and he will be still wiser; teach a righteous man, and he will increase in learning.

ADVANCED WEALTH AND TAX PLANNING CONFERENCE (AWTPC)

Our three-day biannual AWTPC conference is a vital component of the integration-through-education phase of The Better Way. Why you should attend.

1. You will receive approximately 18 hours of hard-hitting, no fluff content.
2. You will receive powerful tools that position you as an expert and the go-to-person in your area.

3. You will receive the mindset, methodologies, and strategies that will make you irreplaceable in the eyes of your most important clients.

4. You will receive knowledge of the latest innovative tax mitigation and wealth planning strategies our clients need and deserve.

5. You will receive turnkey proven strategies to increases your revenues and overall value beyond tax season.

6. You will receive ground-breaking strategies for website productivity that creates enormous value, generate consistence leads, and makes you money.

7. You will receive comprehensive knowledge of the 7-step life-cycle marketing strategy and why you should employ a turnkey automated online marketing system that generates consistent leads through e-mail campaigns.

8. You will receive best practice strategies for attracting, serving and retaining your best clients.

9. You will receive 24 continuing education (CE) credits.

10. You will receive a 100% money back guarantee.

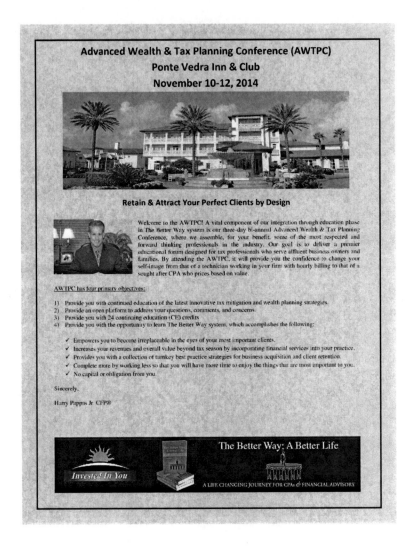

Once the initial education phase is completed, you will have all the necessary knowledge, skills, conviction, and enthusiasm to integrate and operate The Better Way. This phase of The Better Way works under the premise of the old saying, "Tell me, I'll forget. Show me, I'll remember. Involve me, I will understand." Once you truly understand, you will have the confidence to change your self-image from that of a technician working in your firm with hourly billing to that of a sought-after CPA who prices your services based on value. While working within The Better Way, you will have confidence and conviction that you are an essential and indispensable resource for your clients. You now know that you have everything they need to solve their most complex fact patterns.

My research has revealed that accountants get it. They know that being a bean counter is not in their best interest or that of their clients. They want to be proactive, but they just need a system to make it work. CPAs know they must be more proactive to survive during the next wave of the accounting evolution. In order to be viable in the long term, accountants understand and appreciate that meeting clients once or twice a year for tax preparation is not enough. CPAs realize they need to have frequent engagements with their best clients to deliver the services the clients want and deserve. More and more CPAs are incorporating this proactive approach by incorporating The Better Way. Our clients are counting on us to be proactive and to deliver solutions that improve their current situation.

To underscore my conviction of the necessity of a collaborative approach (knowledge hub) to meet the needs of clients, here is a noteworthy quote from Nixon's *Accounting Practices Don't Add Up!*:

> I think networks of firms will play a crucial part in the success of an individual of a firm. Having like-minded yet independent firms working together on client projects and having the ability to "bounce ideas" off each other will be the way of the future. As a multi-disciplinary firm progresses, it will be able to say "yes" to any client situation because of the people hired within the firm or the access to knowledge from their network of firms. Because modern

accounting businesses do not see themselves as competitors to other firms—they believe in growing the size of the pie rather than the size of the slice—they will share intellectual property (through knowledge factories) amongst themselves. The accounting firm of the future will operate more like a bureau service and marketing business and as such, building enduring client relationships will be even more important.

Does Nixon sound as if he is talking about The Better Way? Even the AICPA is getting in on the action by advising its constituents to become the "CPA firm of the future," which entails providing massive value to their best clients, in-house. The solution is The Better Way, an idea whose time has come. It is a life-changing journey in which two firms work together as one toward a common goal, delivering an integrated solution to their best clients within the framework of a strategic relationship built on a foundation of trust and value. If you want to rise above the competition by differentiating yourself, The Better Way will give you that advantage. It is profoundly simple and just as powerful.

ARE YOU THE GO-TO PERSON?

When I have a business issue that keeps me awake at night, the first phone call I make in the morning is to my go-to person. When your best clients have similar concerns, are you on their speed dial as that person? If so, I commend you. I know how much work it takes to get to that position. How about you? Who is your go-to person? If you engage The Better Way, your knowledge hub is that "person."

If you are not your client's go-to person, and that is by design, then that should be of concern to you. If you are not providing exceptional, proactive, value-oriented solutions for your clients, then I propose that you are on the chopping block and will eventually be replaced by a CPA who provides more value to the relationship. Not being the go-to person for your clients is an indication that you are providing a commodity and that your business is at risk.

If you are not the go-to person and that is not by design, then

that concerns me equally as much, as you are giving someone else the value and revenue that you should be earning. What if you had immediate access to a knowledge hub that could be a valuable resource for your clients' complex tax issues? Wouldn't you want to be the go-to person?

If you are the go-to guy and you have a group of people who act as your solution providers (insurance, actuary, money manager, third-party administrator, etc.), are these resources truly the best in their respective specialties? I suspect that what they are really best at is preserving the integrity of the relationship you have built with your client. This is a referral model at its core. I propose there is a more efficient and productive option.

For example, let's suppose that you referred one of your best clients to Bill, who solved a tax problem for that client. Who is likely to be the person your client will brag about to his buddies, you or Bill? That's correct. Bill ends up with a new client and takes all the credit, not you. What if you could have a team, rather than a group, that works with you in a strategic relationship—not a referral relationship? Furthermore, what if you could dictate the speed and the process as well, while having a world-class team working for you and through you? You maintain control of the relationship. All the client sees is you. Now let's assume that same client is talking to his buddies about the tax solution you developed for him. Whom is he now bragging about? That's right. You!

If you are the go-to person and you do it all and it is by design, you must have a large "S" posted on your chest. Do you really believe it is in the best interest of your client for you to be the quarterback, running back, wide receiver, and lineman? Do you really want to throw the ball and catch it, too? How tired are you at the end of the day?

What if we take you off the field and put you on the sidelines as the head coach. Instead of you doing everything yourself (throwing, running, catching, and blocking), imagine having Joe Montana, Walter Payton, Jerry Rice, and other superstars who are the best in their positions play on your team. How much more efficient would you be? How much more valuable would you be?

Why do head football coaches normally wear a headset? They are collaborating with their colleagues in the press box who have a much better view of the playing field. While in the press box, would you not have better visibility, more free time, and potentially better results compared to being on the sidelines? Imagine if you moved from the press box to a blimp. Now you can watch not only one game but also multiple events at the same time. You are high enough to be able to view many activities at the same time. For the system to work, you must stand outside it, observing all the games (fact patterns) from high above. You now can oversee all the moving parts, and control everything from one position. Wouldn't this increase the value of your firm and enhance your company's footprint?

MESSAGE, MEANING, AND MONEY

While working within The Better Way, you play a vital role for your clients and, in our opinion, should be compensated accordingly. There are primarily four compensation methods that CPAs use with The Better Way. It is worth mentioning that some CPAs prefer not to share in any fees or commissions, or they might accept indirect financial incentives such as marketing support and practice-development training.

1. **Value Billing**. A CPA serves as an independent advisor whom clients pay on a fee-for-service basis. The CPA's presence while working with the knowledge hub, via phone and/or meetings, is a valuable asset to the end user. For instance, if the agreed-upon solution for the end user saves him hundreds of thousands of dollars in taxes, should the CPA not charge for the value created?

2. **Hourly fees.** Many accountants prefer to charge hourly fees, mainly because they are accustomed to it.

3. **Percentage of Assets Managed**. This method refers to the previously explained referral or solicitor's agreement model.

4. **Share in commissions**. Unlike a referral fee for assets under management, a commission is compensation for

recommending a product for sale or service to be provided by the CPA or a third party. A CPA who is appropriately licensed to comply with state and federal laws may be paid a commission by, or split a commission with, a licensed agent, agency, or insurance company for the sale of products or services to a client. Usually, the action is a purchase of securities or insurance.

Fee setting is obviously an essential component to all professional service providers as potential integrity issues may occur. Of course, you should simply create a compensation model that is in the best interest of your client, given the value that you provide. As Napoleon Hill once said; "I am convinced that if a man's plans are based upon sound economic principles; if they are fair and just to all whom they affect; and if the man, himself, can throw behind those plans the dynamic force of character and belief in self that grows out of the transactions which have always satisfied his own conscience, he will ride on to success."

CHAPTER 10

The Better Way Business-Building Strategy

The Better Way includes a step-by-step proven strategy for offering new services to current clients, attracting new clients and growing your business. In the end, a successful service business boils down to acquiring and retaining income-producing clients. I suggest that it is paramount to employ a proven turnkey sales and marketing system to accomplish both objectives.

I said them, the two forbidden words in the accounting profession: *sales and marketing*! I know that just the hint of anything to do with selling causes most accountants to cringe, but the fact of the matter is that virtually all of the people who hate salespeople are, in fact, salespeople themselves! I don't care if you are an engineer, coach, teacher, banker, and yes, even an accountant. You are in the selling business. Very similar to financial advisors, CPAs are professionals who must learn to sell and market their services if they want to effectively compete in today's environment.

If you don't believe marketing is essential to a thriving business, I recommend that you be mindful of the words from Hewlett Packard's founder, David Packard, who said, "Marketing is too important to be left to the marketing department." Although some accountants take naturally to selling and marketing, most prefer to take a more humble approach, standing in the background and allowing their work to speak for itself. Marketing a professional CPA firm or financial advisory practice does not have to be expensive, but it needs to be disciplined, focused and monitored. You could be a world-class expert in tax planning, audit, financial statements preparation, or bookkeeping, but when it comes to building a successful business, all the knowledge matters very little. I am suggesting that you go beyond the mere technical aspects of your job as an accountant and begin to think strategically about your accounting pratice.

I don't perceive a conflict between professionalism (accountants) and sales/marketing. They are one in the same, as far as I am concerned. If CPAs are naïve or perhaps overconfident enough to think that they don't need sales and marketing knowhow, I humbly suggest they are mistaken. Maynard Garfield, author of the book *Persuasive Communication: Get What You Want without a Gun,* tells the story of a businessman having trouble selling his ideas. Garfield suggested to the middle-aged gentleman that he should consider taking a course in salesmanship. The man replied, "Son, I will have you know that I have a master's degree in engineering and a doctorate in mathematics. I am not about to subjugate myself to a course in salesmanship. The last thing I want to have anything to do with would be selling. In fact, most salesmen disgust me." Garfield thought quickly and replied, "It sounds like your problem is trying to convince others to accept your advocacies and getting them to do what you want them to do willingly ... Perhaps you could use some help in the art of communicating persuasively. What would you think about taking a course in persuasive communications?" The middle-aged man replied instantly, "Persuasive communications? That really sounds intriguing. Where could I get a course like that?"

Whatever name we give it, however we describe the process, one thing is clear: sales and marketing is unquestionably the heart of any successful business plan. This, among many other reasons, is why I am such a stout advocate that every high school and college student should be required to take courses in salesmanship. The primary lessons that we are taught in school are not the things that carry us through life. Moreover, I have often wondered why schools don't expose teenagers and college-bound students to self-help books. Maybe it is because it is just too real-world for the classroom!

The fact of the matter is that most successful people in any field are the best salespeople. Think about it. They normally have exceptional communication skills, which is a prerequisite. We have to get over the impression that selling is about the slick used-car salesman who hustles people into buying something they don't want, or the pushy, fast-talking peddler who closes folks without them knowing what happened, or that aggressive telemarketer who calls you during dinner to sell you the Japanese steak knives. I propose that we not view sales and marketing as some form of trickery or dishonest behavior. Instead, I submit that we be mindful of the words of authors

Bob Burg and John David Mann in their brilliant book *Go-Givers Sell More:* "Selling is giving. Giving your time, attention, counsel, education, empathy, and value. In fact, the word *sell* comes from the Old English word *sellan*, which means—you guessed it—to give."

"How about this slogan: 'If you are unhappy
for any reason we will feel really bad'."

Yes, indeed. Selling is about giving and caring, not taking. Selling happens when we are engrossed in serving our client. I propose that marketing and selling skills will be the norm for the accounting profession, just as they have been in the financial service industry. Furthermore, I suggest that the most effective way to sell something is not to sell at all, but to honestly care about creating value for your clients. The kind of value that I am referring to is not about just meeting our clients' expectations. I'm talking about going so far beyond that. I am talking about creating the kind of value in which you become primary, critical and essential to your clients. I am talking about the kind of value that is provided before, during and after any type of engagement. I am talking about the kind of value that makes our clients say, "Wow!"

Don't wait until you are paid before you provide value. You are a professional who truly wants to make a difference. Prove to people that you provide value regardless of the circumstances and timing. If you approach sales and marketing with the notion of giving instead of getting and adding value before seeking value, your clients will be astonished with the outcome. I am not suggesting that you become a Mother Teresa. However, I am asking you to faithfully employ the golden rule that you should treat others as you would like others to treat you.

When you create value for your prospects and clients, incredible conviction develops, and you become eager and excited to share your message. For example, let's assume that you truly believe you are, without question, the most ethical and competent CPA in the world, and that no other CPA can offer what you offer your clients (value). Wouldn't it be easy to deliver your message? You would have tremendous conviction, belief, and enthusiasm for what you provide, because you know deep inside that everyone would be better served having you as his CPA. If this were truly the case, would you consider your "message" to be a sales pitch or marketing gimmick? Of course not! So I encourage you to view sales and marketing as not selling but creating value for your client and genuinely caring. You must believe and have absolute conviction that what you have to offer your clients need and want. Accomplish this and it is downhill from there because your conviction and enthusiasm will eventually convert itself into physical action. The words of author Vic Johnson, in his engaging book *Goal Setting: 13 Secrets of World Class Achievers,* is spot on: "Belief is nothing more than what we accept as true or real ... What we accept as true may not be true and it may not be real. But, if we accept it as true or real, it influences our decisions just as if it were." This is why faith is often the spark that ignites the journey to success and significance. What we believe, our mind can conceive.

When you are passionate about the value you bring to the relationship and it is grounded in truth, selling becomes a nonevent. People won't need to be sold. Jay Abraham's insightful book, *Getting Everything You Can Out of All You've Got: 21 Ways You Can Out-Think, Out-Perform, and Out-Earn the Competition*, includes this tale:

> "A farmer wanted to buy a pony for his little daughter. There were two for sale in his town. Both ponies were equal in all aspects. The first man told the farmer he wanted $500 for his pony—take it or leave it. The second man was selling his pony for $750. But the second man told the farmer he wanted the farmer's daughter to try out the pony for a month before the farmer had to make any purchasing decision. He offered to bring the pony out to the farmer's home, along with a month's worth of hay to feed the pony. He said he would send out his own stable man once a week to show the little girl how to groom and care for the pony. He told the farmer the pony was kind and gentle, but to have his daughter ride the pony each day to make certain they got along together. Finally, he said that at the end of 30 days, he would drive over to the farmer's and either take back the pony and clean up the stall—or ask, then, to be paid the $750." Which pony do you suppose the farmer decided to purchase for his daughter?

Darn tootin'! The first man's primary objective is to make a sale, and he is at the mercy of the buyer to accept or reject his offer. The second man's main intention is to add value to someone's life.

When our goal is to add value, we are only dependent on ourselves because when we create value, the money follows. It was Albert Einstein who said, "Try not to become a man of success, but a man of value." I honestly believe that the money I earn mirrors the value I have created, and the more lives I influence, the more wealth I will accumulate. In the end, if I truly focus on the delivery of value, I will become indispensable and irreplaceable to my

> When you are passionate about the value you bring to the relationship and it is grounded in truth, selling becomes a non-event.

clients. Very successful people in the service industry don't just think about themselves. They reflect about what is most important and valuable to their clients because they know that creating value that clients appreciate and want is the best way to receive value in return. Another example of the importance of generating value comes from Mark Anastasi, author of *The Laptop Millionaire*. He explains in his book that successful people are "we-thinkers" and are rich because they add massive value in the world. Employees are not rich because they, typically, use "me-thinking" and, therefore, are more focused on the value that they can get.

I became a student of selling and marketing "value and trust." When I became a financial advisor at the age of 25, I had absolutely no selling experience. However, I always felt comfortable being able to communicate with people at all levels. Additionally, I always worked under the premise of initially providing value to the relationship instead of trying to sell my services. I know that when I feel I am being sold, I am less likely to buy. Why would I want to do that to someone else? Clients want to control the buying process, so let them. I never wanted my clients or prospects to feel I was a hammer looking for a nail. Instead, my intention is never to sell, but to simply help in a way that I would want someone to "sell" me. My goal is to provide honest, useful advice to gain credibility. The more credible I become, the better chance I have to earn the business.

When prospective clients honestly believe that we are truly committed to their success in making the right decision, whether or not we obtain the business, we will be successful. Never forget that the more that we try to sell, the more we act like a hammer looking for a nail! As I mentioned earlier, I never considered myself a salesperson. Some people may refer to what I do for a living as sales, but I call it helping! Furthermore, I suggest that once they change their focus from selling to helping, they too will enjoy sales.

Like you, I am a professional who has a very important message to share that I believe will make people's lives better. All I need is the opportunity to prove it! Additionally, I am convinced that I am the very best financial advisor in the world. I truly believe that! It doesn't matter if it is true or not. It is what I honestly believe. I am absolutely convinced that no other financial advisors care about their clients as much as I do, and that I will always do what is in the best interest of my clients. Because of my belief system, I never feel I am selling. I am simply trying to communicate the value that I bring to the table along with my caring demeanor. You too will have tremendous enthusiasm and conviction when employing The Better Way. You will realize that what you offer is something your competition is not doing. In the end, you will find creating value for your clients is a pleasant experience.

UNIQUE VALUE PROPOSITION (UVP)

In order to stand above the congested tax accounting and wealth-management marketplace, we should offer our prospective and current clients a unique benefit or advantage above and beyond that of our competition. If we are just another "me-too" accounting or wealth advisory firm, what motivation do we give people to consider our services? Perhaps the most important component of marketing ourselves is the unique value proposition, or UVP. According to marketing guru Dan Kennedy, "A unique value proposition is a way of explaining our position against our competition and against all other choices actual or imagined."

In other words, your UVP is the distinct, appealing idea that sets you apart from your competition. I once thought having a UVP was meaningless and served very little purpose. Now, more than ever, I am convinced it's an integral part of what my business stands for. It's how I explain the value I provide to CPAs. I encourage you to develop your own unique value proposition (UVP), your statement of what you do for a living, so that you can sell yourself first.

What's the difference between the next CPA and you? Let's show them how you are different and why yours is the firm they should think about when it comes to tax planning and financial services. When I read the following by author Harvey Mackay in his *New York Times* bestseller *Swim with the Sharks without Being Eaten Alive*, it made me realize just how vital a UVP can be:

- I don't know who you are.
- I don't know your company.
- I don't know what your company stands for.
- I don't know your company's customers.
- I don't know your company's products.

- I don't know your company's reputation.
- Now, what was it you wanted to sell me?

To piggyback off the above bullet points, consultant Leo Pusateri explains that all organizations and teams/individuals in business today need to answer seven simple yet powerful questions to truly distinguish themselves based on their value. Pusateri calls it his "value ladder":

1. Who are you?
2. What do you do?
3. Why do you do what you do?
4. How do you do what you do?
5. Who have you done it for?
6. What makes you different?
7. Why should I do business with you?

I thought the following might lend some support in helping you create your UVP.

THE BETTER WAY UNIQUE VALUE PROPOSITION (UVP)

Who are we?

We are an instrumental back office support system (BOSS) with 28 years of experience that empowers CPA firms to fulfill their purpose, build their brand, and grow their business.

What do we do?

1. Empower CPAs to become irreplaceable in the eyes of their most important clients.

2. Increase accounting firm's revenues and overall value beyond tax season.
3. Provide CPAs with a collection of turnkey best-practice strategies for business acquisition and client retention.
4. Substantiate how CPAs can do more while working less.

Why do we do what we do?

Passion! We have a higher purpose for being in business than simply making money. We believe that if we truly make a difference by becoming a primary, essential, and critical resource for CPA firms, money will follow.

How do we do what we do?

We follow a comprehensive, disciplined, customized, and proven model that provides a competitive edge for CPA firms. Our roadmap to enhanced value (REV) strategy is designed specifically for the accounting industry.

Whom have we done it for?

The Better Way was pioneered in 1997 and has enjoyed remarkable success.

What makes us different?

We eliminate the risk that is inherent in the broken and flawed traditional referral model. The CPA is our "client," not the end user (CPA's client). We don't sell solutions. We sell the CPA to their most important clients. Our way makes their way better.

Why should you do business with us?

1. **Passion.** We have boundless enthusiasm and love for our work. We have a fierce desire to help our clients to achieve their goals.

2. **Commitment.** We have emotional and intellectual commitment to organizational and personal growth. We bring a mindset of innovative learning and dedication to all of our client relationships. We are givers because it's who we are, and therefore, what we do.

3. **Trust.** We earn this coveted distinction due to our clients' total confidence in our abilities, our integrity, and our character. Our clients are confident in us because of our faith in our work and in ourselves. We always do what is right for our clients. We understand and appreciate the importance of an outstanding reputation.

4. **Respect.** We treat our clients, and each other, with the utmost respect. We regard each client relationship as a special privilege. We are constantly considerate, appreciative, and always strive to exceed our clients' expectations.

5. **Value.** We are unique because we know our value and constantly strive to understand our clients' value. We also believe that value is not only the operative word in business today but is the single most compelling word that must be in sales professionals' vocabularies. We are experts at helping organizations to compete effectively using the philosophies of value.

6. **Cost.** Nothing, except your time.

The good news for CPAs is that they don't have to be experts in sales and marketing to succeed in their profession, because in the land of the blind, the one-eyed man is king. To say it another way, you don't have to be a marketing icon to outshine your competition because they are doing such an awful job in this crucial area. I want you to think of yourself as a value creator. I don't want you to think of what you have to say to get people to buy your services. Instead, I want you think about what you can give. True sales and marketing should have nothing to do with shenanigans, or trickery, but everything to do with the value and genuine concern that you have for your client or potential client. When you show value and concern, people will enthusiastically want to patronize your business instead of your competitors' business.

The illustration above is what we affectionately refer to as our Clients for life—I Care Client service model. This proprietary multidimensional approach redesigns the client experience. This model works wonders for my business and can work for you, as well. The magic happens quickly after you unleash this customized, step-by-step method of demonstrating to your clients how much you genuinely care about them and respect them and that you are constantly thinking about their needs. When we position our clients at the heart of everything, while nurturing sincere client loyalty, our clients become less sensitive to price, more forgiving of small mistakes, and, eventually, become our walking billboards. By employing the loyalty-based system, our services become much more than a commodity. Rather, they are built on a foundation of value and personal relationship. It is a "small" difference, but it makes all the difference in the world.

Poor service is everywhere, while great service is rare. Conventional wisdom teaches us to never take our clients for granted, but we are all guilty of this from time to time. Some of us are in violation of the principle far too frequently. Whether they are called clients, customers, constituents, end users or guests, it is imperative that people know we care and that we genuinely appreciate their business and loyalty. To my way of thinking, all people have a profound longing to feel appreciated. Demonstrating appreciation to another person is an enormously overlooked prerequisite in developing meaningful and productive relationships. There have been numerous studies that confirm the number-one reason people leave their jobs is that they don't feel appreciated. It is absolutely paramount that our appreciation be a heartfelt expression of gratitude, and not some kind of fakery that will ultimately come back to hurt us.

When a client fires me (that's right, let's call it what it is), I treat the loss as a tragedy that must be avoided. Virtually every time I am discharged from my duties (that sounds better than fired), it is because I did not invest as much time in the relationship as I should have. Contrary to what many people believe, clients do not fire us because of performance. They terminate the relationship because we took them for granted. We didn't demonstrate our concern and appreciation. If this is the case, we deserve to get the boot!

If we don't invest in our client relationships, then our clients will have no reason not to think twice about experimenting with our competitors. We should never forget that our best clients are our competitors' best prospective clients, and we should always conduct our business as if we were at risk of losing them. If we truly believe our clients are at risk of getting poached by the enemy at any time, then this alone should motivate us to develop and implement a client service model right here and now.

One sure-fire way to place the velvet ropes around our clients is to impress them at every available opportunity. Let's not settle for just satisfied clients. Instead, let's create loyal clients. Let's wow our clients with the best, most rewarding, most fulfilling, and most enjoyable experience we can deliver. If we accomplish this, we should have clients for life.

Check out the results below from the Rockefeller Corporation that studied the reasons for customer defection (2013):

- 1 percent: customer dies.
- 3 percent: customer moves away.
- 5 percent: customer has a friend who provides the same service.
- 9 percent: customer is lost to a competitor.
- 14 percent: customer is dissatisfied with the service.
- 68 percent: customers believe you don't care about them.

In spite of that data, most accounting firms have not invested in developing the core systems, workflows, and infrastructure needed to efficiently provide a consistent level of service for their clients. I am sure they will argue that they are customer focused, but ask them to show you their service model, and you hear crickets! I suggest that most companies treat client service as a low-priority business operation, until there is a complaint. Providing ho-hum service, by merely reacting to client's inquiries, pales in comparison to the power of developing client loyalty through an authentic anticipatory service. Utilizing a reactive client service model seems to be an incredibly inefficient method to produce loyal clients.

FEED THE SEED

It never ceases to amaze me that companies spend millions of dollars to attract new clients (strangers), and spend next-to-nothing to keep the ones they have. The lifetime value of a client is too significant not to employ a service model that provides our clients with an unforgettable and rewarding experience. We must nurture our clients repeatedly and forever. This nurturing process is a multiple contact sport. We never want to give our clients a chance to forget us. Without constant and never-ending communication with our clients, our relationship will likely disappear and so will the money. Mae West had an interesting take on the importance of staying in touch: "Outta sight is outta mind and outta mind is outta money, honey."

Proverbs 27:23—Know well the condition of your flocks, and give attention to your herds.

One of the most crucial threats to our business is our clients' belief that we are replaceable. Due to the advancements of technology and the Internet, many companies are becoming a commodity, while profit margins are being squeezed. If our distinguishing characteristic is that we do great work at a fair price, then how do we separate ourselves from our competitors who sing the same song but at a lower price? We must add value by building deeper and more meaningful relationships with our clients that will help us dodge the threat of commoditization. Here is a gut-check question for you to contemplate: Would your clients be able to describe something unique that you did for them to show that you honestly care and that you are truly different from your competition?

The most compelling resource I read on customer service is Jeffrey Gitomer's *Customer Satisfaction Is Worthless, Customer Loyalty Is Priceless: How to Make Customers Love You, Keep Them Coming Back, and Tell Everyone They Know*. If you want to take your client service to the next level by providing your clients with the most outstanding service possible, I highly encourage you to read this book. Gitomer's no-nonsense approach is packed with wisdom and insights that get to the heart of the matter quickly and effectively. Gitomer asks, "Would you rather have a satisfied spouse or a loyal spouse? Then, would you rather have satisfied customers or loyal customers?"

I love the following reminder about how quickly we can go from hero to zero: "I am a nice client who never complains and never comes back. You know me; I am a nice person. When I get lousy service, I never complain. I never kick. I never criticize, and I wouldn't dream of making a scene. I am one of those nice clients, and I will tell you what else I am: I am the client who doesn't come back. I take whatever you hand out, because I know I am not coming back. I could tell you off and feel better, but in the long run, it is better just to leave quietly. You see, a nice client like me multiplied by others like me, can bring your business to its knees. There are plenty of us. When we get pushed far enough, we go to one of your competitors."

If you are looking for a goldmine of best practice ideas to strengthen trust between you and you clients, I suggest you pick up a copy of Andrew Sobel's *All for One*, in which he says, "Like a healthy living program, cultivating your relationships is not a one-off event, but rather a lifestyle. This is no longer an individual game, but rather a team activity. You need to tirelessly reinforce a collaborative, client-centered culture so that everyone's actions are motivated by one for all and all for one." In his delightful book *Don't Worry, Make Money*, Richard Carlson makes a statement that rings true to my ears: "As long as our expression of gratitude is genuine, other people love it and remember it. This not only makes them feels good, but it also encourages them to help us again and to encourage others to do the same." Rather than being just another accounting firm, servicing clients indiscriminately, why not develop a strong, tightly defined client retention system to make you the best game in town?

As mentioned previously, there is a sea of sameness (SOS) among accounting and financial advisory firms. We all appear to do the same things in the same way. If we want to stand out in our profession and not go the way of the dinosaur, then we must market our firms and develop skills to sell our services. If we want our clients to stay, pay and refer, then we must offer the highest caliber of advice and service by adopting a team approach that embraces the highest level of integrity to meet our clients' needs and demands. I am not saying this will be stress-free. What I am revealing to you is that it will be worth it!

BECOMING A LOYALIST

In a threatening, competitive, and price-sensitive environment, client service is one of the most critical means to separate us from our competition. I argue that client service should not be just a so-called department. In its place should be a business philosophy that is entrenched in everyone on your team. Our service philosophy incorporates a loyalty-based methodology that offers proven best practices for designing and implementing an incredible client experience. If something is essential to our clients, then it is integrated into our model. Our approach is extremely personalized on the outside, but exceptionally well automated on the inside.

If you read any of Michael Gerber's E-Myth books, you know his core premise is that a business should be constructed and systemized as it would be franchised. A case in point is Amazon.com. In online commerce, there is Amazon.com, and then there is everybody else. Amazon's knack for generating loyal customers is amazing to witness. Its customer service is highly impressive. It has everything down to a science. It's no secret around the office or my family that I am an Amazon junkie! I perform virtually all of my online shopping via this astonishing, word-class, online retailer. It is a client-focused, efficient, fast, easy, no-hassle, and, of course, free-shipping type of company! Could I get my merchandize cheaper at other retail outlets? Possibly, but I don't care, because I love the customer experience and Amazon's commitment to quality customer care. It has converted me from a satisfied customer to a loyal customer. The reason that Amazon has the best in customer service is that the company truly cares about its customers and wants them to partake in an incredible shopping experience, one they have never before experienced. I read that CEO Jeff Bezos always has an empty chair next to him during his important customer-service meetings. The vacant chair is there as a reminder to everyone in the meeting who the most important person in the room is: the customer. Everything is performed with the customer in mind. Now, does it surprise you why Amazon has millions of loyal customers like me?

By comparison, I am reminded of Lily Tomlin's character Ernestine, who uttered those famous words on Rowan & Martin's *Laugh-In,* "We don't care. We don't have to (snort). We're the Phone Company!" Sadly, this type of customer service behavior is still commonplace in today's environment. These individuals and companies they represent feel just as Ernestine did. AT&T once controlled almost all local and long distance telephoning in America and figured it could do as it pleased. Developing loyal clients was not even on the radar for the company. It was too busy counting its money to worry about developing and implementing a customer-service model.

"I'm sorry, he's not available. Can you call back when you're more important?"

Proverbs 11:25—A generous person will prosper;
whoever refreshes others will be refreshed.

"I CARE" CONCEPT TO CLIENT LOYALTY

My core belief regarding client service is to give more than what we are paid for, and some day we will be paid more than we give. Does that sound a little like the law of reciprocity mentioned earlier? It's all about going the extra mile, which Napoleon Hill defined as "rendering more and better service than that for which one is paid; and giving in a positive mental attitude." The key to delivering the Wow! experience is to remember the following:

1. It cannot be self-serving. It's not about us.
2. It must be personal.
3. It must be unexpected.
4. It must be frequent.

Proverbs 3:3—Never let loyalty and kindness leave you!
Tie them around your neck as a reminder.
Write them deep within your heart.

The foundation of a successful client service model is demonstrating to our clients how important they are to our business, and that they are valued and cherished. When this is successfully accomplished, we provide a gift to our clients that is similar to placing a value on food, water, or air. It is priceless. When we truly care about demonstrating to our clients that we genuinely care about them and we can complete this initiative in a systematic and efficient manner, we have a pow-

We should never forget that our best clients are our competitors' best potential clients, and we should always conduct our business as if we are at risk of losing them.

erfully effective client retention system that cements our client relationships. We should regularly ask ourselves the simple question of whether our relationships with our best clients are truly as robust as they could be. If we honestly answer no, then it behooves us to do something about it. If we can answer yes to the question, then we have clients who see us as irreplaceable and extremely valuable and, most importantly, who will tell their friends and family about our amazing advice and service.

© Randy Glasbergen
glasbergen.com

"I don't know how he does it, but that salesman
always makes me feel like I'm the center of the universe!"

There is no immediate and easy approach to developing loyal clients. However, there is a lengthy but incredibly effective approach to cultivating clients for life! Because loyalty takes time to develop, most people don't engage in a system to bring it to fruition. Instead, these short-cutters are seeking a quick fix and are not interested in any time-consuming technique to take their clients from satisfied to loyal. Loyalty manifests itself day by day. It is a marathon, not a sprint. When it is all said and done, a business that concentrates its efforts on delivering the most value to customers and generating the most trust receives the greatest rewards. I propose that our clients will judge us on the following three items:

1. The value we add
2. The degree of trust we acquire
3. The extra mile we go

I often hear my colleagues and business associates argue that client loyalty no longer exists. I beg to differ. I suggest that clients have no reason to be loyal. We can't expect clients to be loyal when all we do is just our job. We must go over and beyond the call of duty to prove to our clients that we are critical and essential to their business and personal success and that we genuinely care about them. Let's not forget why many consider a dog to be the best salesperson ever. That's right, good ol' Fido. He is the only animal, including man, that doesn't have to work for a living. A hen lays eggs, a cow gives milk, but a dog makes his living by showing a genuine interest in others.

CHAPTER 11

Needle-Moving Best Practices

B elow are just a handful of best practices that The Better Way employs.

MONTHLY CLIENT NEWSLETTER

One of the best ways of establishing consistent client contact is through a printed client newsletter. In fact, I would go as far as to say that this is a must-have for growing one's practice. My four-page monthly color newsletter is the silver bullet that has allowed me to expand my practice and develop loyal clients. I know that many professionals claim they receive poor results from newsletter services and that is because they are doing it the wrong way and for the wrong reason. First of all, a newsletter should be used to build trust and loyalty with your clients, not to sell products or service. This is not the givers gain mentality. Our objective with our newsletter should be to build loyalty with our clients. It cost me about $300 a month to produce and mail my newsletter and I am telling you right here and now it is worth every penny. Moreover, virtually everyone I know uses the canned, off-the-shelf newsletters, for which someone else provides the content, which is usually dry and boring. On the other hand, when you send a customized, personally written, well-crafted newsletter to your clients, it can be a very powerful tool. My news-letter became successful when I learned to communicate with my clients in my own voice, rather than using a canned approach. I have spent the past 25 years writing my personal "homespun" newsletter, and I know my clients look forward to reading it, because hundreds have told me so. I truly believe if we are not arriving at our client's mailbox (not e-mail) with a custom newsletter, we are missing a tremendous opportunity to build meaningful relationships. Okay, let's dispel a big myth right now. Writing your own newsletter is not difficult; it just takes time and discipline. We all know what it is like to read boring stuff and we know how nice it is to read engaging and thought-provoking copy. It isn't rocket science. Just put stuff in your newsletter that you would want to read and you will be golden.

I find it remarkable that so few professionals write their own newsletter. When I ask them why, I get the same answers just about every time; no time, too hard, I can't write, and not sure the bang is worth the buck. What is interesting, they all agree that my custom-ized approach is better than the canned approach. Some say I ain't paying $3,500 a year just to build loyalty. Ouch! Now that hurts. It is a shame that these folks are missing an enormous opportunity to build loyalty with their best clients. I encourage you not to be one of them!

Below is an example of a CPA newsletter that we produced.

VIDEO E-MAIL FOR BUSINESS
E-MAIL ON STEROIDS

This is a relatively new addition to my tool chest and I absolutely love it and so do my clients and prospects. The video e-mail really sets me apart from others. I don't know any other advisor or CPA that utilizies this relatively inexpensive service. It is ridicuously easy to set up and it integrates seamlessly within Outlook.

All you need is a simple web cam on top of your PC and follow three simple steps:

1. Create it: This is the recording
2. Review it: If you don't like it. Delete and start over
3. Send it: When you hit the send button your Outlook window appears and you send it like any other e-mail

You can even track it! You will receive an e-mail when your client or prospect watched the video.

Another neat feature with this service is that it comes with sample templates or you can private label your own like I did (see below). I pay $49 a month. If you plan to purchase the service let them know you got the referral from me and you should receive a discount.

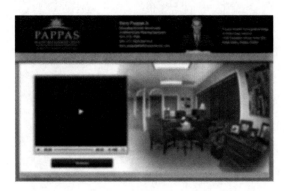

YEAR-END CLIENT VOICE SURVEY

This is arguably one of the best strategies that I have ever implemented for my business and for the past dozen or so years I have not employed this amazing best practice. My firm prohibts sending surveys at the risk of receiving an uncomplimentary comment, which could be considered a complaint. Need I say any more? One of the most crucial activities for a professional service firm to employ is an annual client survey, which I refer to as "year-end client voice." I learned a long time ago that the secret to talking is listening, and if we ask enough of the right questions, then our clients will tell us how to improve. Said another way, if we want to help someone, then we should shut up and listen! Unfortunately, too many folks simply don't listen well enough or they don't provide clients the chance to talk. The foundation of your Client for Life I Care client retention system should be your year-end client voice assignment. I am not referring to the typical, corporate, pat-on-the-back type of survey forms that don't get to the root of any potential problems. I suggest that they are nothing more than an exercise with no substance, carried out in the hope of convincing clients their service provider cares. The truth of the matter is that clients see right through these shallow questionnaires. Instead of companies measuring loyalty, they seek satisfaction. Measuring client satisfaction only proves that everyone did what they were supposed to do. That means diddly squat (technical term for *very little*). People get a pat on the back for just doing their job. If a client is satisfied, I am doing a mediocre job. I want loyalty, not satisfaction. We need to ask the tough questions, the ones that get to the real truth of the matter.

> We want and need to hear from our unhappy clients, as they are our greatest source of learning.

The right questions separate the achievers from the sustainers. If we want an accurate and truthful report card, then let's ask candid and straightforward questions.

I am not surprised at the results of a 2010 CCH Accounting Firm Client Survey showing that most CPA firms fail to seek formal feedback from their clients. According to the survey, most CPA firms do not have a prescribed system for gathering opinions of clients. Forty-eight percent of business clients and just twenty-one percent of individual clients reported receiving a formal client satisfaction survey from their CPA firm in the past year. It's surprising that, given the importance of client retention today, firms are not measuring client loyalty in a formal way. If our clients can tell us how to improve, then why would we not want to listen? We can't be so naïve to think they will tell us when they are unhappy. Numerous studies confirm that most people will not voluntarily give feedback, good or bad.

Most service providers are forever complaining that clients are more demanding, less forgiving, harder to satisfy and less loyal than ever before. As odd as this may appear, this strikes me as huge opportunity for us to grow our business! Why? Because it becomes much easier to acquire new clients. In other words, if everyone were content with our service, why would they consider changing firms? However, when clients are disappointed, upset and frustrated, they are more likely to change providers. This is what makes the annual survey remarkably potent. We need to play offense, not defense. We need to be out in front of any potential problems, not waiting for them to present themselves and then move into crisis management mode. When we eventually acquire this "demanding" new client, it's our job to have systems in place to make our new client less demanding, more forgiving, easier to satisfy, and more loyal. Yes indeed, in every adversity lies the seed to opportunity!

We want and need to hear from our unhappy clients, as they are our greatest source of learning. Negative feedback is really just an improvement opportunity. Furthermore, soliciting feedback from our clients demonstrates that we genuinely care and want to improve the services and advice that we offer. Although I am a proponent of a more in-depth client survey, you may want to consider the following simple approach if you want to use the excuse that surveys are too time consuming. Send a simple letter to your clients asking two questions:

1. On a scale of 1 to 10, how do you rate our business relationship?" If less than 10, please answer the next question:

2. What would it take to get to 10?

© 2007 by Randy Glasbergen.
www.glasbergen.com

"The bad news is, our customers hate us. The good news is, we have a lot fewer customers than we used to!"

Imagine what we can learn from those questions. We need to listen, learn, and apply. If we don't earn a 10, then we must know what is required to get there. What I find fascinating is that when companies survey clients, they often ask about additional services clients would like from their firm. It's common for the feedback to include services the firm already provides! Do you think these firms have a marketing plan in place? Heck no! Do you know what the best-kept secret in town is? A CPA firm that offers financial planning and asset management services! Do you know the worst thing a CPA wants to hear? "I didn't know you did that."

This client survey issue reminds me of a charming story about a young man who walks into a drug store and asks the pharmacist if he can use the phone. He dials a number and asks the party who answers if the number is correct. Once he learns that it is, the young man says, "I would like to apply for a job as your gardener ... oh, you already have a gardener? Is he a good gardener? You are not planning to make any changes, are you? Well, thank you anyway." The young man hangs up the phone, and as he leaves, the pharmacist says, "Son, don't be discouraged. You will find a job." The young man turns and, looking confused, replies, "Who's looking for a job?" The pharmacist said, "I overheard your conversation asking for a job as a gardener." Smiling, the young man says, "Oh, no, sir. You see, I am the gardener. I am just checking to see how I am doing."

Proverbs 15:31– If you listen to constructive criticism,
you will be at home among the wise.

The most important component of the year-end client voice survey is how we respond! If we do not show an honest and genuine effort to make good on the clients' requests, suggestions, and so on, then we will cause more pain than gain. It is absolutely critical that we demonstrate to our clients that we truly value and appreciate their business. This is not just an exercise; we must take this assignment seriously. I advise that you not make the same mistake that so many others have when they obtain vital and critical information from clients and then do nothing with it. You must develop and implement a client retention strategy in your practice with the ultimate goal of creating loyal, not just satisfied, clients. Our clients will continue to support our businesses if we give them a reason to be loyal. Client loyalty is worth rewarding!

WEEKLY E-MAIL MARKET UPDATES AND LINKS TO POPULAR ARTICLES

Every Saturday morning, I prepare the weekly market wrap-up. I add a weekly quote, cartoon, and links to the most-viewed financial articles of the preceding Friday. This is not sent as an attachment. Instead, it is a template that displays in full view when clients open their e-mail.

Private label banner

My photo

Quote

Cartoon

Market Summary

Links to news stories

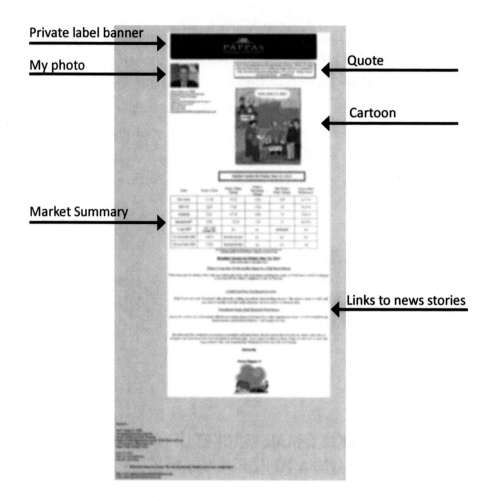

"NOTABLE NUMBERS" WEEKLY E-MAIL

"Notable Numbers" is a weekly e-mail consisting of 13–15 interesting and thought-provoking bullet points of quick and timely facts relating to the financial and tax service industry. This is a superb way to stay in touch with clients while providing them with something that they truly enjoy reading. As you can see from the two photos on the next page, you are able to private-label the weekly information to suit your needs.

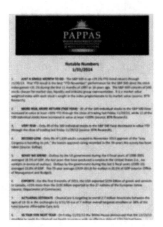

MMFI INITIATIVE

Everybody wants and needs to feel valued and appreciated. Our Make Me Feel Important (MMFI) initiative is a never-ending pursuit to demonstrate to our clients just how important they are to us. Sincere praise and appreciation are rare and precious commodities. As Mark Twain said, "I can live for two months on a good compliment." Below are a few of our MMFI projects with excerpts from actual letters:

- **Personalized thank-you letters to choose from.** The two most cherished words are *thank you*. The two most neglected words are *thank you*. We must make a conscious effort to regularly send thank-you notes, letters, and cards to our most cherished clients. In *The Pursuit of Wow!*, Tom Peters said the thank-you note is the most important advice he has to offer and just about impossible to beat!

Dear Harry and Vickie,

*I hope this letter finds you at a good time and ...
I am sending you this note to simply say ... I want
you to know how much you ... Clients like you
have enabled me to thrive in this business for 25
years. It is important for me to take time out of my
busy day to stop and give thanks to those I value
most. You have my heart-felt gratitude for your
business and our great working relationship. As
you well know, the past 19 months has proven to
be one of the most challenging environments in
recent memory. It is important for you to know
that you have a well-diversified, prudent and
cost-effective investment strategy. Casey, Lisa,
Sally, and I will continue to do everything possible in order to give you the service and investment advice that you want and deserve. Please
don't ever hesitate to call us with any questions,
comments or concerns. We look forward to
winning your confidence all over again every
time you call us for advice or service.*

- **Personalized wedding anniversary letters to choose from.**

Dear Ron and Doris,

*Happy nineteenth wedding anniversary! Mar-
riage is a wonderful and beautiful commu-
nion ... Unfortunately, it has taken a beating ...
Quietly, with little fanfare, a broad and deep
body of scientific literature has been accumu-
lating that ... In virtually every way social sci-
entists can measure, married people do much*

better than the unmarried or divorced ... How
big a difference does marriage make? If David
Letterman were to compile a Top Ten list for
marriage, it might look something like this ...

- **Personalized new client anniversary letters to choose from.** On the anniversary of the account opening, our clients receive a personalized letter commemorating the day we established our relationship. It is essential that clients know we are thinking of them on this very special day, a milestone in our business relationship. We want clients to know that we don't take our relationship for granted and that we will never forget the day they placed their trust and confidence in us.

  Dear John and Lois,

  January 2, 2014 is a ... It is the beginning of our
  seventeenth year ... I am sending you this letter
  to simply say ... I want you to know that there are
  few people I ... and I am extremely fortunate to
  ... Your loyalty means more to me than what ... I
  clearly recognize that you have virtually ... when
  selecting someone to assist you with your ...
  Thank you for always believing in us ... are dedi-
  cated to demonstrating our sincere appreciation
  for your patronage by providing you ... with the
  very best service and prudent investment advice
  ... to do everything possible to maintain your
  loyalty. We don't ever intend to ... disappoint
  you. Valued clients like you, John and Lois ...
  have allowed me to succeed ...

  Cheers!

- **Personalized Thanksgiving letters to choose from.**

  Dear Jack and Jane,

  Happy Thanksgiving! Although each of us has experienced our own challenges and blessings in life, I believe it is our adversities ... The real secret in Thanksgiving is to give thanks ... People that find and acknowledge the fundamental good in their lives, even when it is obscured ... As I sit with my family for Thanksgiving dinner, I will count ... I cannot thank you enough for your continued loyalty. It means more to me than anything you might imagine. In addition, I will be thankful for my ... I sincerely hope that your Thanksgiving is the start of a pleasurable holiday season, and the prelude to a brighter ...

- **Personalized Merry Christmas/Hanukah letters to choose from.**

  Merry Christmas Harry!

  While searching for the right words for my annual Christmas letter, I came across a funny cartoon that I thought you would enjoy. There was a picture of a woman ... noticed the slogan, "Keep Christ in Christmas" on a sign ... Even the churches are sticking their noses ... The Christmas season is upon us. A period in which there is so much care and concern ... Too often in the hustle and bustle of the season ... trappings of the holidays and forget there is a spiritual meaning ... but service and love. It is the most precious gift of all, Jesus Christ. The Bible tells us in John 3:16, "God so loved the world that He gave His only begotten Son, that whosoever believes in Him should not perish, but has everlasting life." For many folks, Christmas ... People are uniting with ... For others, it is a time of sorrow ... They may suffer from the humiliation ... The presumed "best time of the year" will not ... Instead, it will be a time of loneliness ... To help promote my desire, I have enclosed a $25 Wal-Mart gift card along with a ... kindness card. While performing an act of thoughtfulness, provide ... card to the recipient. It is the hope that the receiver will then use the card to "pass it on!" In addition, you may want to invite the person to Jesus' birthday party! The invitation is below ...

- **Personalized birthday cards to choose from.**

  Happy Birthday, Vickie!

  May your special day bring to you all things that make you smile ... yesterday's memories, today's joys ... As you know, old people and the problems associated with getting older are the subjects of many jokes. While these funny stories ... us folk who are now approaching the age of those in the jokes to laugh ... side of life. I hope the following old age jokes bring you smiles, laughs and ... for God's gift ... Looking at getting older with humor ... Life may not always be a ... but laughter means that there ... Through humor, we can soften some of the ... Remember, "He who laughs, lasts!"

STRATEGIC, DYNAMIC, AND INTEGRATED

The previously discussed best practices (except for the survey) are what I am using right now. I refer to these type of services as random acts of kindness (RAK) efforts. I am not selling aything. In its place I am simply creating value and showing that I genuienly care. Again, these RAKs are just a few of the hundreds that I employ to differentiate me from others.

I encourage you to proceed with caution when providing "boilerplate" type gifts. Instead, focus on personalization (go the extra mile) to demonstrate that you have invested time and money to show your sincere appreciation for the trust and confidence that your clients place in you. Another quick example of a RAK is, the next time you read a good book, think about what client would enjoy the reading and then send them a copy.

Let's always think how we can add more value and make our client's lives easier and more interesting? There is no such thing as a static relationship. We are either becoming closer or further apart when trying to maintain and nurture our client relationship. Customers will continue to patronize those businesses that give them a reason to be loyal. Customer loyalty is worth rewarding.

Remember that danger is in the distance. Let's always stay close and continue to feed the seed.

Proverbs: 11:24—There is one who scatters,
and increases yet more. There is one who withholds
more than is appropriate, but gains poverty.

CHAPTER 12

The Mysterious Unknown Knowns

There are two critical questions for you to consider: Do you see the need to change how you are operating your practice currently? Do you recognize what possibly could be ahead for you if you don't make changes?

The brutal truth is that there has been an onslaught of information and irrefutable evidence that suggest if you don't make significant changes very soon, you could be left so far behind your competition that you might think you are actually in first place! You may want to think again if you are one of those who continue to ignore signs of an unpleasant outcome if changes are not made.

It is clear that the CPA practice is undergoing a shift in focus, in which CPAs now realize that they need to find ways to provide a much higher level of service for their best clients who are demanding more. Clients understand that you and I can't be experts in every subject matter, but what they want is the assurance that we have assembled a team of experts to work with us to solve their problems.

For the past several years, the accounting profession has been warned repeatedly about what it will take to become an accounting firm of the future. Accounting firms are reminded of how technology will continue to commoditize compliance, creating significantly diminished value for traditional accounting services. There is little doubt that compliance revenue will continue to plunge, while value-added services will be the way accounting firms of the future earn the bulk of their revenue. The fact is, far too many accountants are engrossed with tax returns and audits instead of creating real value for their clients.

I suppose there is enough discomfort to persuade CPAs that a change is essential, but the real pain is coming! It has been said that the number of accountants entering the financial planning field during the early '90s could best be described as a trickle that has become a flow and will soon be a torrent. When the flood arrives, the pain will be so great that, regrettably, it may be too late to make the necessary changes. If you are starting to feel the pain, then I encourage you take the leap of faith into a robust new opportunity, expanding your horizon and implementing The Better Way system into your practice.

The business graveyard is littered with cadavers that simply ignored the evidence of an imminent structural change in their industry. I call this the "unknown knowns of change." It is analogous to knowing what should be done (known), but not acting on it for some unknown reason. You may recall the following famous words of Secretary of Defense Donald Rumsfeld in his the statement of February 12, 2002, at a press briefing: "There are known knowns; there are things we know that we know. There are known unknowns; that is to say, there are things that we now know we don't know. But there are also unknown unknowns. There are things we do not know we don't know."

I suggest it is the "unknown knowns" that are most disruptive for businesses that are trying to innovate. For instance, let's imagine something that you know is true. This represents the "known." Now think of something that you know is in your best interest (true), but you don't act on it. This is the unknown. For example, a client of mine asked me to review his company's ten-year-old life insurance arrangement (buy/sell, etc.) to see if there were areas for improvement. Keep in mind that the CPA and an insurance agent initially implemented the insurance program. One would think that a CPA knows that he should occasionally review his client's insurance policy to make sure it is adequate in the current environment. This is the "known." Although the CPA knows this to be true, for whatever reason, he does not act on this truth. This is the "unknown." In other words, it is unknown why the CPA knows the truth but does not act on the truth. This is where folks make a big mistake; the unknown known! We don't get hurt by what we don't know. Instead, we get hurt by what we know and don't do.

> When new circumstances present themselves, we can either cooperate with it by learning how to benefit from the change or we can resist the change and eventually get run over by it.

When new circumstances present themselves, either we can cooperate by learning how to benefit from the change or we can resist the change and eventually get run over by it. It's our choice. The challenge lies in a willingness and dedication to shifting your paradigm from the role of technical advisor to strategic business advisor. The process doesn't have to be overwhelming. It is often said that the secret to getting ahead is getting started. I suggest that the secret to getting started is breaking the issue in question into small, manageable tasks, and then attacking each minor task one by one. If you begin the transformation one task at a time, you will be on your way to seizing the opportunity to become the CPA firm of the future.

Nevertheless, when push comes to shove most people fail to engage because of six self-imposed roadblocks.

1. No time
2. No money
3. No belief
4. No passion
5. No concern
6. No courage

The obstacle that gets my blood boiling the most is "no time." People will find time for things they care about! Period! Over and out! When people say they have no time, what they are really saying is that this is not a priority for them. So let's just call it what it is. Let's not rationalize, make excuses or point fingers. The fact of the matter is people are simply resistant to change. They are amateurs who need to consider turning pro.

"TURNING PRO"

As author Steven Pressfield so brilliantly stated in his thought-provoking book *The War of Art*: "It's one thing to lie to ourselves. It's another thing to believe it. Rationalization is resistance's spin doctor. Its job is to keep us from feeling the shame we would feel if we truly faced what cowards we are for not doing our work." Resistance stops us from living out our purpose and passion. *The War of Art* suggests a strategy to bring the fight to this stubborn enemy. Pressfield calls it "turning pro." When we go from an amateur to pro, amazing things begin to transpire, but turning pro is terribly difficult because resistance is a force of incredible influence and power. It manifests itself in fear (aka anxiety, self-sabotage, avoidance). When we are courageous enough to make the transition from amateur to pro, we no longer rationalize and, more importantly, we declare a perpetual war on the enemy (fear) and bring resistance to its knees.

The primary reason Pressfield's message resonates with me is that I believe, without question, that my ability to fight through resistance and take action is what separates me from most folks. I am not one who is without fear. I simply have the wherewithal to succeed in spite of it. The pro plays hurt. Nelson Mandela's words sum it up nicely: "The brave man is not he who does not feel afraid, but he who conquers that fear."

As Pressfield so eloquently explains in the *War of Art*, "The amateur believes we must first overcome fear; then he can do his work. The professional knows that fear can never be overcome." I feel it in my gut. I know it can defeat me on any given day as easily as the need for a drink can overcome an alcoholic. I afford it the utmost respect because I know there is no such thing as a fearless warrior. We all fight fear and resistance every day, but instead of yielding to it, we fight it and continue to go narrow and deep with our purpose and passion. Sure, we will get bruised from time to time, but the pro plays hurt. He simply takes a few Advil and FIDO! On the other hand, the amateur chooses distraction in the face of uncertainty. As Pressfield cleverly states: "Amateurs tweet; pros work." He further sums up the life of the amateur: "In the end, people either have excuses or experiences, reason or results, buts or brilliance. They either have what they wanted, or they have a detailed list of all the rational reasons why not."

In the end, the difference between an amateur and a pro is in their habits. Many people comment about my ability to maintain a highly disciplined and structured schedule. People think I am naturally disciplined. Nothing could be further from the truth. Yes, I am disciplined and I maintain strict habits, but nothing is natural. Just like most people, my rational mind wants a fabulous beach body, but my emotional mind wants the chocolate chip cookie. I fight the temptation every day with my emotional mind, but I believe in myself and I am willing to pay the price to break through the roadblocks to become the person that I want to be. This is not nearly as difficult as accepting the consequences of an undisciplined lifestyle with poor habits.

THE ELEPHANT AND THE ROPE

In the book *How to Effectively Market and Manage an Accounting Firm,* author Romeo Richards makes a thought-provoking comparison between our beliefs and our limitations. Richards tells the fascinating story of a baby elephant in captivity. A small rope tied to one of its legs is affixed to a small wooden post in the ground to prevent the elephant from roaming. The elephant is confined to an area determined by the length of the rope. The baby elephant tries to break the rope, but it can't. After a few attempts, it stops trying, resigned to the fact that it cannot break the rope. When it grows up into a 1,000-pound creature, it can easily break the rope, but it never even tries, believing that it still can't. As the author describes, many of us are like the 1,000-pound elephant that does not know its power. You have the power and wherewithal to take your business to levels that you never dreamed of. You must believe and change from the mentality of the baby elephant to realize you can indeed break the rope.

By integrating wealth-management services into your practice, along with a proven, turnkey, step-by-step innovative business model, you will be able to exceed your client's expectations and position your firm to outpace your competition. More and more

CPA firms are beginning to wake up to the fact that they must do more for their best clients. Studies have shown that one out of two CPAs will offer financial services in the future to remain competitive. A recent study that was published in the CPA Journal titled *Accountants & Financial Planning: Structure for Success* estimated that over the next ten years an additional 6,600 accounting firms nationwide will offer financial planning services. The same study estimated that between 65,000 and 90,000 of the 400,000 members of the AICPA currently offer some level of financial planning services. Over the last four years, the number of AICPA members who earned the personal financial specialist (PFS) specialty designation, which is available only to CPAs, has doubled in the past two years and tripled in the past three. Another indicator of the trend is the expansion of events such as the AICPA's Implementing Personal Financial Planning conference, which became a stand-alone event for the first time in 2012. The writing is on the wall and it is unmistakably clear. There is a boatload of substantiation that points to the necessity of becoming more proactive or risk going the way of the dinosaur. Don't become another casualty of the unknown known!

ARE YOU THE MAN IN THE ARENA?

Below is an excerpt from a speech by Theodore Roosevelt, titled "Citizenship in a Republic." He delivered his address in Paris in 1910. This extract is now titled *The Man in the Arena*. The meaning of the speech is that it is better to attempt to do something with all your heart and fail than to be a spectator. The man in the arena is the person who is deeply involved in a situation that requires courage, skill, or tenacity, as opposed to someone sitting on the sidelines and watching:

It is not the critic who counts; not the man who points out how the strong man stumbles, or where the doer of deeds could have done them better. The credit belongs to the man who is actually in the arena, whose face is marred by dust and sweat and blood; who strives valiantly; who errs, who comes short again and again, because there is no effort without error and shortcoming; but who does actually strive to do the deeds; who knows great enthusiasms, the great devotions; who spends himself in a worthy cause; who at the best knows in the end the triumph of high achievement, and who at the worst, if he fails, at least fails while daring greatly, so that his place shall never be with those cold and timid souls who neither know victory nor defeat.

This brings to mind the critic who, deep inside, hears a voice that says, "If I had any guts, I would do it myself instead of criticizing those who are trying." Folks, we have to suit up and take some blows, as that is the price we pay to be a participant and not a spectator. What's paramount is that we must recognize that being the man in the arena, getting trampled by the bull, is far better than playing it safe in the stands. I put forth that people who fail in business and life are regularly the ones who think they have it all figured out. They are stubborn in their ways and are virtually untouchable and they find it terribly difficult to be receptive to new ideas and better innovations. Frankly, I find this a welcome advantage for those of us who recognize that learning is an everyday occupation. They become a sponge, soaking up everything they can find that could potentially provide them with ways to improve, both personally and professionally. To learn and grow in life, we must want to improve and be teachable. This requires listening to those who have earned the right to speak, who have already accomplished what we are trying to do.

CHAPTER 13

What We All Want: More Time, More Happiness, More Money

My steadfast dedication to my business and long hours at the office have led many to infer that my family and personal life is neglected. This is far from the truth. Hard work and long hours doesn't necessitate misery and divorce. I continue to work about ten hours a day and a few on weekends, but virtually all the rest of the time is devoted to my wife and kids. I don't believe one's family needs to pay a price for one's success. We simply need to set our priorities and keep the first things first.

I must confess that including the following few pages was an incredibly difficult decision for me. As you may remember from the preface, I mentioned my reluctance to use this book as a platform to discuss my spirituality. But without this chapter, this book would not be complete. Living a God-centered life and understanding and applying Scriptures to my daily activity has been instrumental to my success in business as well as my personal life. Having God as the center of my life has helped me keep my business endeavors in proper perspective and to declare that getting to the top does not require transformation into a ruthless, Gordon Gecko-like creature.

Back in the day, success to me was like a carrot on a stick: every time I got close to it, it moved. I soon realized that being prosperous by industry standards did not satisfy my appetite. After I became successful, I wanted something more. I kept telling myself that I would be content someday, instead of being content and happy along the way. I was not grateful for what I had. I was more focused on what I did not have. I didn't get it that it is virtually impossible to be grateful and unhappy at the same time. In other words, as long as my heart is focused upon what I don't have and upon what I think I need or am entitled to, happiness will elude me.

It took me far too long to appreciate that career success is how people who care about me the least evaluate my worth as a person. I always thought that a better version of me was the answer. My pastor refers to this as "the cul-de-sac of stupidity." As crazy and sad as this may appear, I once looked upon spirituality and religion as being something that would soften me up and leave me complacent. I was fearful that if I became more peaceful, content, and relaxed, then I would suddenly lose my edge, and my compulsion to reach my goals would disappear.

TURNING POINT: MY DARK DAYS

The toughest battle that I ever fought was in 2004, when my life came to a grinding halt due to a treatable medical condition: clinical depression. I went off the grid for about six years. This beast shook me to my very core and destroyed my sense of purpose in life, as my mental, emotional, spiritual, and physical faculties were all but gone. I was emotionally bankrupt and stuck in gut-wrenching agony from an unrelenting illness. Shortly before I was diagnosed, I became increasing irritable and short-tempered. As time went by, I began to feel worthless, could not make simple decisions, and lost my joy for work and family. I felt I was the loneliest person in the world. My passion and commitment was gone. I had no future, a crushed soul, and a broken heart, and things were getting worse by the day until things started spiraling out of control. I never thought I would ever be happy again and then, one day, I could not get out of bed, couldn't go to work, and couldn't do anything. I just physically couldn't! I didn't have an appetite and quickly lost 20 pounds. I had no energy or care to do anything except lie in bed and sob uncontrollably. Then the panic attacks arrived, along with persistent insomnia. I now knew why people committed suicide. This was unbearable.

> I read somewhere that we repeatedly turn to God for help when our foundations are shaking, only to learn that it is God who is shaking them!

Although I understand and accept that pain, suffering, stress, and other difficulties are the admission tickets to the game of life, I literally thought I was going crazy. Everything seemed pointless and hopeless. The more I thought about my condition, the worse it seemed to get. I thought my life, as I knew it, was over. Nevertheless, I fought through my toughest moments. I had no choice. I simply used the tools and mindset that I employed in my business to get me out of this awful dark hole. I wish I could say that my road to recovery was a straight line. Sadly, it was a slow roller-coaster ride of lows with only a few highs. It was a sluggish and painstaking grind for six years. I thought about giving up many times, but a wise man told me that it was okay to think about giving up; just don't do it.

While I was fighting the war, I repeatedly heard a small voice deep inside my soul that regularly whispered, "You can do it. Keep fighting.

Stay strong. Believe in yourself. This is just another adversity that you will overcome and be better and stronger because of it. You will have an amazing woe-to-win story to share that will make a difference in someone's life."

It is hard to put my pain into words for those who have never experienced the torment of clinical depression. As I type these lines, my fingers shake with every key I touch and a terrible sinking feeling enters my stomach, while disturbing, vivid images appear, reminding me just how bad it was. Fortunately, with God's grace; wonderful doctors; steadfast support and love from my wife, children, family, friends; and my dogged determination, I was able to endure and conquer this horrible monster. Unfortunately, many people regard depression as a personality weakness or character flaw. Some consider it to be akin to a scarlet letter, a mark of shame. It is estimated that 90 percent of depression sufferers don't seek treatment because they want avoid the risk of an embarrassing stigma. It was different for me. I welcomed discussion of my health condition with anyone who would listen and offer support, as I was desperately seeking a light in my sea of darkness. I am convinced that my six-year debacle was a wake-up call to help me recognize what is most important in life. Moreover, I argue that failures, roadblocks, and adversities are placed in our path for a good reason: to guide us in the direction that we are meant to go.

I have learned that adversity awakens us to the treasures that are far more important than money and material possessions: our health, our families, and our friends. Sudden financial losses teach us that we should not base our happiness on money. An illness teaches us to be humble and lead a healthy life. Regrettably, oftentimes it takes a major tragedy for me to be reminded that I need to better appreciate what I have and to quit taking things for granted.

Nevertheless, I am happier now than I have ever been in my life. I discovered that trusting God with the mysteries of suffering is often the answer to the problem of suffering. I read somewhere that we repeatedly turn to God for help when our foundations are shaking, only to learn that it is God who is shaking them! M. Scott Peck in his book *The Road Less Traveled* said, "Once we truly know that life is difficult—once we truly understand and accept it—then life is no longer difficult."

To expound on this point, *The War of Art* author Steven Pressfield made another wonderful observation in his book:

> The moment a person learns he has terminal cancer, a profound shift takes place in his psyche. At one stroke in the doctor's office, he becomes aware of what really matters to him. Things that sixty seconds earlier had seemed all-important suddenly appear meaningless while people and concerns that he had until then dismissed at once take on supreme importance. Maybe he realizes working this weekend on the big deal at the office isn't all that vital. Maybe it's more important to fly cross-country for his grandson's graduation. Maybe it isn't so crucial that he has the last word in the fight with his wife. Maybe instead he should tell her how much she means to him and how deeply he has always loved her. Superficial concerns fall away, replaced by a deeper more profoundly grounded perspective.

Could it be said any better?

"You only live once. But if you work it right, once is enough."

—*Comedian and singer Joe E. Lewis, 1902–1971*

I now surround myself with the success climate of Scriptures and really learn to know God and let him guide my mind and spirit. As a result, I have enjoyed substantially more peace, tranquility, and yes, productivity. Not only am I living a more God-centered life but, also, I'm as productive as ever as a financial advisor, father, and husband. I now know that success is a process, not a destination. It is something you experience gradually over time. Placing God at the epicenter of my life was not easy; it took a lot of effort, just as building my business did.

As we all know, no amount of money can provide health, happiness, and, certainly, eternal life. In fact, I believe many wealthy people long for something money can't buy. I used to think how lucky people were to be rich. I used to think they had it all. Of course, this is foolish thinking because I now believe that most wealthy people who do not have God in their life are really quite unhappy on the inside. It is a shame that so many people are wealthy in the physical sense, but bankrupt emotionally and spiritually. Make no mistake. Rich people are not always happy people. Indeed, I have learned that a person's value lies not in anyone's apparent importance, or possessions, or net worth. No, true value over and over again lies with the handicapped, the sick, and the poor. I have learned far more from these folks than I have from the wealthy.

Many years ago, someone told me something quite profound: "You will go out and make a lot of money and most likely become very wealthy. You will most likely buy material things, but one day you will meet someone who simply does not care how much you have in material wealth and then you realize just how poor you are." A new study analyzing the relationship between wealth and happiness concludes there is no such relationship. "The evidence is that we get richer and richer but we don't get any happier," observes

Robert Skidelsky, economic historian and coauthor of a book on modern capitalism, titled *How Much Is Enough?* The basic goods that compose a happy life include health, education, leisure, friendship, and harmony with nature, according to the author.

Having more money is important to most people, but I argue that more *time* is what we all really want. We all want more time to live so that we can enjoy the things that are most important to us. To some of us, money is the most important thing, but you still need time to spend it. It is suggested time and again that if we just do more—do more work, see more people, make more calls, set more appointments, sacrifice more, compromise priorities more—then we will earn more money. I agree, but at what price? As we know, money is powerful. On one hand, it allows people to reach their dreams, while at the same time it becomes a nightmare for so many others. The overwhelming majority of people who have accumulated wealth will tell us flat out that they did not become more blissful as they accumulated more wealth. Money does not equal happiness. Over and out!

If you are like me, you struggle with creating proper balance between work, family, friends, hobbies, and God. I argue that it is a significant challenge for everyone. Skidelsky said, "A good life is a life that contains these basic goods and once you've got enough money for those, you have enough—so to carry on working for more is silly." I submit that most people are far more impressed and affected by people who have a passion for serving others, not by the amount of money they accumulated. I thought the following words of wisdom from Alexander the Great and President Woodrow Wilson would prove to be a real eye opener in our age of materialistic abundance and a befitting way to conclude this chapter.

ADVICE FROM ALEXANDER

While lying on his deathbed, Alexander the Great summoned his generals and told them he had three final wishes:

1. The best doctors should carry his coffin.
2. The wealth he had accumulated should be scattered along the procession to the cemetery.
3. His hands should be severed and hung outside the coffin for all to see.

One of his generals, surprised by these unusual requests, asked Alexander to explain. Here is how Alexander replied:

- I want the doctors to carry my coffin to demonstrate that, in the face of death, even the best doctors in the world have no power to heal.

- I want the road to be covered with my treasure so that everybody sees that material wealth acquired on earth, stays on earth.
- I want my hands to swing with the wind, so that everyone understands that we come to this world empty handed and we leave empty handed when the most precious treasure of all is exhausted: time.

WISDOM FROM WILSON

President Woodrow Wilson was in his first term in the White House in 1913 when he uttered these words while speaking to the students of Swarthmore College. "You are not here merely to make a living. You are here in order to enable the world to live more amply, with greater vision, with a finer spirit of hope and achievement. You are here to enrich the world, and you impoverish yourself if you forget the errand."

Although speakers and authors have used this quote for over 100 years, as I understand it, most people do not fully appreciate President Wilson's intent. I sure didn't until I read Dr. Larry Markson's book *Talking to Yourself Is Not Crazy: Change Your Inner Dialog, Take Control of Your Life,* in which he provides a superb analysis of this historical passage:

> First, "You are not here merely to make a living," and while the vast majority of uninformed people do not know that, it is the bitter truth. They believe that making a living is what it is all about, and nothing could be further from the truth. Just making a living is survival thinking at best and indicates relegation

to a lifetime struggle just to keep up. Merely making a living generally indicates a mediocre existence, a "sameness," a safe routine with nothing changing over time—a stuck-in-your stuff attitude. Surely, just getting by does not scream of the excitement, happiness, fulfillment or energy field that comes by setting high standards, lofty goals and taking massive action steps. Remember, we were born to look up, look ahead and move forward.

The next sentence of Woodrow Wilson's quote, "You are here in order to enable the world to live more amply, with greater vision, with a finer spirit of hope and achievement" seems to me to be self-explanatory, except for the fact that it is sneaky powerful. When we break it apart a bit we find, "To enable the world to live more amply," which is a phrase that speaks of universal potential, of abundance and of generosity.

And how about, "With a greater vision," which has always been and always will be the key to success, positive change and growth. A vision, a concept, an idea or future thought that when put into action creates targets that result in expansion and new applications.

That sentence ends with Wilson saying, "With a finer spirit of hope and achievement" which is truly the magic of the sentence because without hope all is lost. Hope stirs the pot of human potential by saying that there is a dream of more, of bigger, of better.

There is a chance to grow, for things to get better and for achievements that while they may not be possible at the moment are inevitable in the future.

And finally, Wilson ends with, "You are here to enrich the world, and you impoverish yourself if you forget the errand." Yes, you are here to do your part, to contribute and to enrich, not only yourself and others, but to make larger more altruistic contributions to humanity at large—to share, to give back to the source and to something greater than yourself, to help, to venture forth, to love!

"And you impoverish yourself if you forget the errand" is the lesson of the universe. It says that, either you are expanding or shrinking, moving forward or backward, giving or taking—and, in case you forget to do that as part of your mission in life, you will end up poor of spirit, of mind, of body and of purse.

Yes, yes, yes—"You are not here merely to make a living. You are here in order to enable the world to live more amply, with greater vision, with a finer spirit of hope and achievement. You are here to enrich the world, and you impoverish yourself if you forget the errand."

If President Wilson were alive today, I hope he would offer me his wink of approval for a job well done. Although I undoubtedly make a living from my profession as a financial advisor, I am enriched by the errand of serving others.

CHAPTER 14

Your Future Is Not Today but Today Could Make Your Future

"What if we don't change at all ...
and something magical just happens?"

I gave it my best effort to motivate and inspire you to consider a new way of doing business. The secret to getting ahead is getting started. Is now that time? The time to take action? The time to quit thinking about your old practice? The time to start imaging your new business? The time to seize the opportunity? When there is an opportunity to truly make a difference, the mindset of "possibly someday" isn't found in companies that are determined to differenti-ate themselves from their competitors.

When opportunity presents itself to forward-thinking companies to provide exceptional service to their best clients and to position their firm for the future, they seize the opportunity. In their book *Everyone's a Coach*, Don Shula and Ken Blanchard suggest that learning is defined as a change of behavior: "You haven't learned a thing until you take action and use it." Action is what conquers fear and anxiety. Remember that there are three kinds of folks:

1. Folks who make things happen;
2. Folks who let things happen;
3. Folks who wonder what on earth happened.

The people who make things happen are masters of change. The other two are usually its victims. Regrettably, the people who will not pay the price to change end up paying the ultimate price for not changing. Even so, I know that making the leap into the unknown can be a scary proposition and overwhelming. Typically, we make changes when we feel the need to or are forced to change. For instance, many people want to stop smoking, but they don't feel they need to until after they have a heart attack. In other words, people change when their need for change becomes greater than their desire to remain content with what is known. There are many ways to go forward, but only one way of standing still. Waiting is standing still. Not deciding is standing still.

DANGER IS IN THE DISTANCE

We all have experienced the phenomenon of how easy it is to stay in motion once we have started the motion, but if we stop the motion, it is extremely difficult to get the motion going again. I refer to this as "danger in the distance." This concept applies to all aspects of my personal and business life. I know with tremendous certainty that the more time (distance) there is between what I should be doing and what I am not doing, the more difficult that endeavor becomes. The longer I wait (distance), the tougher it becomes to do the right thing. I will not allow distance to come between me in exercise, diet, client service, reading or whatever. If I allow distance to grow, there is no doubt danger is coming. My motto is to never start stopping and never stop starting. I bet you read that one again! Think about it. It makes sense. I'll let Confucius give my final arguments on the importance of never stopping: "It doesn't matter how slowly you go as long as you do not stop."

If you genuinely care about your future and want to do something meaningful with it, then you should give careful consideration to incorporating The Better Way. As I have said repeatedly throughout this book, without application, virtually everything we learn is useless. Author and speaker Denis E. Waitley, said that most people spend their entire lives on Fantasy Island, which he calls Someday Isle! In other words, someday I'll do that. Someday I'll change. So how do you bridge the gap from knowledge to action? Perhaps the answer is with this formula: (K + F = A). **Knowledge** fueled by **Faith** equals **Action**. You need to believe (faith) that taking action is the correct decision.

> My motto is to never start stopping and never stop starting.

Proverbs 14:23—In all labor there is profit,
but mere talk leads only to poverty.

PLAYING IT SAFE INSTEAD OF
PLAYING IT WITH PASSION

The road that takes you to the next-generation accounting firm is perhaps a long one, and no, it isn't scenic. In fact, taking this expedition will require making necessary modifications to your business model and necessitate significant understanding and support. You have arrived at the familiar fork in the road and the route you take could easily characterize the rest of your career. Most people prefer to choose the visibly safe path, which will take them back home to their comfortable and secure place of regularity.

Traveling down the other route will require faith in the unknown, but the trip offers the potential to witness something really exciting, different, significant and truly enjoyable. During your trip down the unfamiliar trail, you will have the opportunity to produce the beans instead of just counting them; create the future of your clients, instead of just reporting on the past; build a much sought-after place to work, and create a go-to place to address your clients' challenges; have young accountants excited about working for a technology-savvy and value-adding accounting firm, instead of loathing to work for the traditional unadventurous and monotonous company.

You can choose the road that will conceivably transform a sleepy, uninspired CPA firm into a powerhouse. I am not an oblivious optimist and this journey is not a pipe dream. It is within your grasp if you are willing to step out of your comfort zone and look into the exciting future of accounting and wealth-management services.

Virtually all of the greatest success stories arise after people become willing to go off the main road and attempt something that was unfamiliar to them.

What route did Amazon's founder and CEO Jeff Bezos travel? In his 2010 Baccalaureate Remarks, "We Are What We Choose" at Princeton University, Bezos encouraged graduate students to take risks, follow their passions, and make choices with compassion as they embarked on the next phase of their lives after Princeton University:

> Tomorrow, in a very real sense, your life—the life you author from scratch on your own—begins. How will you use your gifts? What choices will you make? Will inertia be your guide, or will you follow your passions? Will you follow dogma, or will you be original? Will you choose a life of ease, or a life of service and adventure? Will you wilt under criticism, or will you follow your convictions? Will you bluff it out when you're wrong, or will you apologize? Will you guard your heart against rejection, or will you act when you fall in love? Will you play it safe, or will you be a little bit swashbuckling? When it's tough, will you give up, or will you be relentless? Will you be a cynic, or will you be a builder? Will you be clever at the expense of others, or will you be kind? I will hazard a prediction. When you are 80 years old, and in a quiet moment of reflection narrating for only yourself the most personal version of your life story, the telling that will be most compact and meaningful will be the series of choices you have made. In the end, we are our choices. Build yourself a great story. Thank you and good luck!

© Randy Glasbergen.
www.glasbergen.com

"IT MAKES NO SENSE TO WORRY ABOUT THE FUTURE.
BY THE TIME YOU GET THERE, IT'S THE PAST!"

Maintaining the status quo should not be an option for us. The world will pass us by. Let's not leave our future behind us. I chose and continue to travel down the roads less traveled, trusting that it would lead me in the right direction. Although things have worked out better than I ever expected, the journey was not without lots of adversity and disappointment. Frankly, I don't believe you can have one without the other. It has to be tough or everyone would do it. I hope that what I have demonstrated to you will help you significantly reduce your learning curve, creating more success sooner than expected.

Proverbs 3:5-6–Trust in the Lord with all your heart,

and lean not on your own understanding; in all your ways

acknowledge Him, and He shall direct your paths.

If you are ready to turn pro, move past the potential roadblocks and seize the opportunity presented. I urge you to get involved with a team of like-minded people. You deserve a team that converts rhetoric into results by walking their talk. They must practice what they preach. In other words, they don't proclaim, "Do as we say, not as we do." They must live their message by providing you with a competitive edge in the form of a comprehensive, customized, proven and unique process. Your team must have the right professional experience so that you avoid the learning curve that many CPAs face when adding financial services to their practice.

Although your team must be uniquely positioned and qualified to help you, you need to believe in yourself first. If you have that belief and you are interested in taking your success to an entirely new level, roll up your sleeves and get to work with your team.

Here is another engaging story about believing in yourself, told by *Swim with the Sharks* author Harvey Mackay:

> The class of 30 molecular biology students had assembled to take what would be a grueling final exam. But to their amazement, their professor made them an incredible offer once they were all seated. "I know how concerned you are about your grade point averages and the pressure of being accepted into medical school," the professor said. "And since I am convinced you fully understand the material we have covered this semester, I will offer a B to anyone here who would prefer not to take the final exam." Once the students got over the shock of this offer and realized it was in earnest, a few of them arose, thanked the professor, and departed. During the next few moments, so did a number of others—until only seven students remained. "Anyone else?" the professor asked. The seven remained seated, so the professor closed the door, and passed out the

exam. It consisted of three sentences: Congratulations! You have just received an A in this class. Keep believing in yourself and good luck.

In his stunning book *Golden Rules, the Lost Writings*, Napoleon Hill suggests that you simply need to apply the R2A2 formula. The R2 stands for *recognize and relate*, and the A2 for *assimilate and apply.* The A2 part of the formula is the most important, because if you don't apply what you have learned, it becomes just an exercise. The opportunity to step out of your comfort zone is here, right now. I encourage you not to be a spectator watching life happen around you or the amateur who has exciting plans for his business and life, but they all get implemented tomorrow. Instead, let's say yes to the unknown, yes to uncertainty, yes to fear, and yes to a unique challenge. Comfort is an illusion, a fantasy that imagines freedom from pain, and suffering if we only stay still and avoid change. What most fail to realize, typically, until it's very late in the game, is that change happens to us whether we like it or not.

BACK TO *JERRY MAGUIRE*

Beyond "Show me the money," the movie's most amusing and touching scene may be when Jerry Maguire pleads to his one and only client, the narcissistic Rod Tidwell, to help him understand how he can help Tidwell. "Help me help you," Jerry Maguire begs repeatedly. His client replies that he's looking for more than a big payday. He wants love, respect, and sense of community that only a true partnership can foster.

"Help me help you" are four simple but powerful words that define what many people need and are seeking but often don't ask for. Please allow me to express that to you. As entertaining as it might be, I'm not going to follow you into a locker room and act out a dramatic plea for help. However, I honestly believe if you allow me to help you, remarkable things should happen for you, me and most importantly your clients.

When you tap into the power of The Better Way, you will begin to behave differently by forming new productive habits. Your enthusiasm and conviction will influence others. You won't have to fake a smile or rehearse your body language because your enthusiasm will guide your delivery and others will experience their own Aha! moment. For the most part, the reading is over. Are you content with mediocrity or do you want to accomplish something profound? Do you want the odds stacked in your favor? Do you want an edge? Do you want to break down the barriers to your success? Do you want more freedom to enjoy life? I propose that The Better Way can make your way better. Give it a try.

WELCOME TO THE WINNERS CIRCLE: ENGAGING THE BETTER WAY MY FINAL WORDS

"I regret that my poor choice of words caused some people to understand what I was saying."

So here we are near the end, or are we at the beginning? If you happen to be one of the fortunate few who are committed to making things happen, then I submit that a lot of work needs to be done. I remain ready. Are you?

As I mentioned throughout this book, we are committed to providing a world-class experience for every one of our clients (CPAs) and their clients (end users). In order to maintain our high standard of service, we are very selective regarding the firms we engage with. It is critically important that we connect with CPAs who share our vision and mission, even if that entails regularly turning away business. It is paramount that we participate in a mutually beneficial business relationship founded on trust and value. We will not engage in any transaction that does not benefit all whom it affects, and we will not become the go-to firm for companies that do not fit our defined core business model. As they say, it is much more difficult to get out of a bad relationship than into one.

The Better Way client is the CPA who is the go-to person for his best clients. Additionally, we will not spend our time and money on a firm that wants to experiment. We look for the "all-in" mindset so that we can develop and maintain relationships with those who share our values, beliefs, and passions with respect to expanding their existing tax practice with a holistic, wealth-management integration process.

Before we make our decision to partner with a CPA firm, we initiate a series of exploratory meetings that are described in the first few steps of "Anatomy of an Integrated Model." The primary purpose of this initial meeting is to answer one fundamental question: are we a good fit? Both your time and ours is extremely valuable, so the meeting is designed to help us determine as quickly as possible whether or not an affiliation should be considered.

During our initial meeting, we give you our complete attention, to learn and understand how you are doing business and if there are any kinks in your armor. We help identify any inefficiency in your business model and spend time discussing the potential for a better you. If we mutually agree that the juice is worth the squeeze, we will spend time developing a relationship that is built on trust and value. In the end, we take the value that we bring to the table and integrate it into your current business model in order for you to apply it in a way that is best for you and your clients.

As much as we would like to employ The Better Way with every CPA who is a good fit, I realize this is essentially impossible, especially if you are located too far from Jacksonville, Florida. While a long-distance relationship is possible, it may serve you better to seek the services of a local financial advisor who employs The Better Way model. Anthony Lombardi trains about 100 advisors a year from around the country. We may be able to locate an advisor who is closer to your office, if that would make it more convenient and practical for you. Please do not let my location deter you from having the courage to take your first big step. Simply send me an e-mail or give me a call to get the ball rolling.

Is your future in front of you or behind you? If it's in front of you, then let's take action. Let's begin our venture. Let's get into the nitty-gritty. Down and dirty. Let's live out our dreams while others dream out their lives. This can be accomplished by getting involved with The Better Way. I stake my reputation on it!

I truly hope this book has created an epiphany for you and that you recognize there is a better way: The Better Way, A Better Life. In the final analysis, The Better Way approach is like a hammer and a bunch of nails. You can build a doghouse or a castle. It is all up to you. I strongly suggest that you choose the pain of discipline over the pain of regret. Let's stop waiting for permission to move forward. It ain't coming. Give yourself permission now!

As we approach the end of this journey, I hope our paths will cross again soon. In the meantime, I wish you the very best as you unleash your potential to become the CPA firm of the future. If you forget everything I have said, please just remember *to work diligently, master your subject, create value for your clients, and serve them passionately.*

Finally, do you remember Dicky Fox, the older man in the movie *Jerry Maguire*? He had a heart-warming, no-nonsense philosophy on selling, business, and life. I love Mr. Fox's words near the end of the movie: "I don't have all the answers. In life, to be honest, I have failed as much as I have succeeded. But I love my wife. I love my life. And I wish you my kind of success." My sentiments exactly!

Harry Pappas Jr., CFP®
www.thebetterwayabetterlife.com
harry@thebetterwayabetterlife.com
904-473-4915

Work diligently, master your subject, create value for your clients, and serve them passionately.

Pappas Media Group LLC
822 A1A Highway North
Suite 310
Ponte Vedra Beach Florida 32082

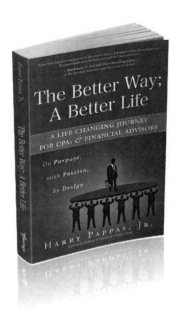

How can you use this book?

MOTIVATE

EDUCATE

THANK

INSPIRE

PROMOTE

CONNECT

Why have a custom version of *The Better Way; A Better Life?*

Build personal bonds with customers, prospects, employees, donors, and key constituencies

- Develop a long-lasting reminder of your event, milestone, or celebration
- Provide a keepsake that inspires change in behavior and change in lives
- Deliver the ultimate "thank you" gift that remains on coffee tables and bookshelves
- Generate the "wow" factor

Books are thoughtful gifts that provide a genuine sentiment that other promotional items cannot express. They promote employee discussions and interaction, reinforce an event's meaning or location, and they make a lasting impression. Use your book to say "Thank You" and show people that you care.

The Better Way; A Better Life is available in bulk quantities and in customized versions at special discounts for corporate, institutional, and educational purposes. To learn more please contact our Special Sales team at:

1.866.775.1696 • sales@advantageww.com • www.AdvantageSpecialSales.com

CPSIA information can be obtained at www.ICGtesting.com
Printed in the USA
LVOW12s0034020514

384089LV00010B/22/P